*A remarkable liberal approach to post-Christian faith.*

If you're ready to let go of limiting theological assumptions about Jesus and open your heart directly to meditative communion with God, this book will prove of great help in expanding your personal relationship with the divine.

**Also by John Selby**
*Seven Masters, One Path*
*Quiet Your Mind*
*Let Love Find You*
*Sex and Spirit*
*Fathers: Loving Them*
*Kundalini Awakening*
*Conscious Healing*
*Meditation: The Cool Way to Calm*


**Author's Web Site:**
**www.johnselby.com**

# JESUS
## for the rest of us

## John Selby

HAMPTON ROADS
PUBLISHING COMPANY, INC.

Cover design by Jane Hagaman
Cover art © royalty-free/Corbis

Hampton Roads Publishing Company, Inc.
1125 Stoney Ridge Road
Charlottesville, VA 22902

434-296-2772
fax: 434-296-5096
e-mail: hrpc@hrpub.com
www.hrpub.com

If you are unable to order this book from your local
bookseller, you may order directly from the publisher.
Call 1-800-766-8009, toll-free.

Library of Congress Cataloging-in-Publication Data

Selby, John, 1945-
    Jesus for the rest of us / John Selby.
        p. cm.
    Summary: "Drawing on his research of meditation and his lifelong work as a thera-
pist and spiritual counselor, former minister John Selby shows how to nurture the
love and guidance of Jesus in our lives. Going beyond the prevailing debate and
dogma, he introduces a Jesus that we can bring into our hearts through the meditation exercises he provides"--Provided by publisher.
    ISBN 1-57174-475-4 (pbk. : alk. paper)
    1. Bible. N.T. Gospels--Meditations. 2. Bible. N.T. Gospels--Criticism,
interpretation, etc. 3. Jesus Christ. I. Title.
    BS2555.4.S45 2006
    232.9--dc22
                        2005034848

ISBN 1-57174-475-4
10 9 8 7 6 5 4 3 2 1
Printed on acid-free paper in Canada

# Dedication

With much love and remembrance, I dedicate this book to my mother, Mildred Selby Smith, who nurtured in me a questing mind and loving heart that she set free to rove beyond her own beliefs, so I could discover my own unique engagement with spiritual reality. In like spirit, I also dedicate this book to my father, Walter Smith, a cattleman who taught me to look beyond cultural games and religious assumptions, to see the truth clearly – and act on it. I am also deeply thankful to my childhood minister, William Gearhart, and his daring challenges to Presbyterian theology; and his wife, Lucille, who quietly walked the universal heart path and touched so many hearts and minds in the process. May the spiritual advances and insights of our new generations respect and build on the wisdom and sincerity of those who have come before . . .

# Author's Note

I'm well aware that this book will upset traditional Christians and Bible-thumping fundamentalists – because I do intend to raise issues that used to get people burnt at the stake. But the purpose here is not to argue theology, nor to question the deep spiritual experiences with which many Christians continue to be blessed. This discussion is for those who no longer find traditional or right-wing Christian theologies and practices fulfilling, and wish to put aside constricting beliefs in order to be free to explore the direct meditative experience of Jesus' presence and guidance in their lives.

Thomas Jefferson stated bluntly, "I do not find in Christianity one redeeming feature." I don't go quite so far in this post-Christian approach to Jesus and his meditative teachings. Beyond the often-dreadful history and fear-based theologies of the Christian Church, the more contemplative and mystic qualities of Christianity have sustained deep spiritual experience in millions of hearts. I am writing this book to put aside the influence of the

Christian priestly cult, so that we can freely explore the enduring power of Jesus' continuing spiritual presence in our lives.

We are living in a period where a large and growing number of people consider themselves post-Christian, in that they no longer believe the traditional Christian dogma of their parents and grandparents. This book presents a new spiritual vision and meditative process grounded in the nontheological experiential dimensions of Jesus' teachings. Through regularly employing this post-Christian meditation process, you will gain the power to move beyond limiting religious programming and enter into your own unique communion with the divine.

# Contents

# Introduction

# Throwing Out the Baby . . .

The date was May 7, 1972, and the location just 12 miles north of Golden Gate Bridge, at the San Francisco Theological Seminary, where I'd done my graduate studies to become a Presbyterian minister. I was sitting in a small stone room waiting to enter a larger interrogation room where 12 somber, black-robed Presbyterian ministers were set to conduct an official inquisition into my beliefs and future in the church. At my side, serving as my nonofficial advisor for the religious trial was the then quite famous (and slightly notorious) philosopher and writer Alan Watts. He was 50 years old and I was 26; he was my primary father figure at the time, as well as my meditation teacher.

He glanced at me and grinned. "John," he said, in his crisp British accent, "just remember what Jesus told his followers to do when they were brought before the authorities."

I stared at him a moment – then I remembered Jesus' challenging advice:

When they bring you before the rulers and authorities, don't be anxious about what you will say – at that very hour the Holy Spirit will come and teach you what to say.

"Uhm," I said, "that's a pretty risky defense strategy."

"Not really. Just stay in your heart, stay with your breathing," he advised. "Allow events to happen – there's a higher good at work here."

Moments later, I walked into the interrogation room and faced the 12 authority figures who had assumed the power to judge me. If they found my beliefs in violation of church theology, they could kick me out of my job as minister and even remove me from church membership entirely. For over two hours, I was grilled with questions probing my beliefs, my faith, my religious attitudes and actions. I had been accused by the senior pastor of my church in San Rafael of several supposed heresies: of teaching Buddhist and Hindu beliefs in my Bible-study group; of secretly teaching my youth group hatha-yoga and Tibetan Buddhist meditation; and furthermore of advising a woman during a counseling session to let go of her belief that she was a hopeless sinner needing Jesus to die on the cross to save her from eternal hellfire.

To top it all off, a Bible of mine had surfaced in which I'd gone through the New Testament and highlighted in yellow all the sayings I felt certain in my heart that Jesus had said, and blacked out all the sayings I attributed not to Jesus but to theological additions of the early disciples and editors.

This was, of course, blasphemy in the Presbyterian Church – how dare I edit the words of the Bible! For weeks I'd been preparing a foolproof theological argument to prove that my unusual approach to Christianity wasn't blasphemous but was, rather, a new approach to being a Christian. My mind was full of loads of quotes from the Bible and from great Christian theologians to support my argument. But when I opened my heart and allowed Spirit to speak through me – oops! – none of that head-tripping argumentative defense emerged from my lips.

Instead I surrendered to a good powerful feeling inside as I stated honestly that my grounding as a Christian had less to do with anything written in the Bible and more to do with direct spiritual experiences of Jesus and God that came to me during meditation. I loved the mystic and contemplative dimensions of church history, and I used the Bible mostly to find clues to lead me into a deeper communion with God. I just wasn't interested in theology per se because theology meant "thinking about God" rather than opening one's heart to experience God directly.

The judges weren't liking what they were hearing. One of them proceeded to give me a short lecture about how the foundation of Christianity was the written logical Word of God in the Bible, not vague feelings in the heart, which could be induced by the devil just as easily as the Holy Spirit. They questioned me further, especially about a seminary paper I'd written called "The Priestly Cult in Religious History," a rather inflammatory paper in which I'd hotly attacked the tendency of historical religious leaders to rule through fear, judgment, and power plays rather than through love, acceptance, and humble service.

> Yes, I answered honestly, I did feel upset that my own Christian religion's priestly cult had ordered the execution by bonfire of over seven million women during the Inquisition, simply because those women refused to believe what the priests demanded.

Furthermore I was upset that, with the Vietnam War currently raging, most Christians were supporting the war rather than speaking against it. Jesus had said very clearly to turn the other cheek and love one's enemies, while the church rallied to the violent cause of its newest holy war against nonbelievers. I was young, I was upset, I spoke my heart.

Finally, I was quizzed on conversations I'd had with various people in my church about Maria Magdalena and her relationship with Jesus. I knew I should hold my tongue on this topic especially, but I found myself instead expressing what I felt strongly: that the Christian tradition was perpetually patriarchal and seriously unbalanced, and the only solution, as I saw it, was a resurrection of Maria Magdalena to a position of spiritual prominence equal to that of Jesus.

A couple of years previously I'd personally experienced a vision late one night at seminary (which I'd written down the next morning and which the tribunal now had a copy of as most damning evidence) in which Jesus and Magdalena were lovers and equal spiritual partners.

> I admitted to the 12 judges that yes, when I meditate and open my heart to Jesus' presence, I often also feel the presence of Maria Magdalena as the balancing feminine half of the spiritual team.

This single-handed transformation of the totally masculine Christian trinity into a mixed-sex four-part spiritual party was, of course, considered absolute heresy. The 12 black robes had heard enough. They retreated to consider my case. I sat there with a strange sense of calm acceptance, and wasn't at all upset or even surprised when the tribunal ended with a formal declamation that I had been judged as follows: According to church doctrine, not only was I not to be considered or accepted as a Presbyterian, I wasn't even a Christian, but rather some heathen Buddhist Hindu pantheist refusing to accept Jesus as my Lord and Savior.

Therefore, henceforth by declaration of the tribunal, I had no right to call myself a Christian. I was to be denied Communion and removed from my position as minister, with my name stricken from the church list of true believers. I was, for all intents and purposes, excommunicated from the church.

## Life on the Outside

What a shock – to be suddenly given the formal boot out of the beloved flock. All my life, my church circle and community had been central in my social routine and sense of belonging. Now, suddenly, I was banished from the circle – unless I would repent, change my beliefs, deny the spiritual reality I knew in my heart, and bow down to the men in black.

"Strange," I told Alan afterward over a glass of what he called our celebration wine, "I'm no longer a Christian, but I still feel Jesus' presence in my heart."

Alan raised his glass with a grin. "You spoke the truth and the truth set you free. Welcome to the Outsider Club – you'll actually find it much more interesting."

Well, for a while, I did miss the sense of belonging to an extended group. I'd wake up Sunday mornings and feel a bit lost. But as the weeks and months went by and I plunged into a new life as an intern at the fledgling American Film Institute, intent on writing spiritually imbued screenplays, my inner experience deepened into realms I'd never imagined.

It was such a great relief to finally feel free to believe (or not believe) whatever I wanted. For the first time in my life, I was able to explore whatever spiritual experience came to me, without fearing that I'd violate beliefs to which I was supposed to dogmatically adhere.

I also did something most people do when they get kicked out of a group. I got mad at the church and all things Christian, closed my heart to everything associated with my religious upbringing, and plunged into other religions, especially Buddhism. I even denied the value of mystic experience in the Christian tradition, claiming that, like Thomas Jefferson, I found nothing to redeem church history.

Basically, I threw the baby out with the bath water and for several years closed my heart to the inner relationship I'd had with

Jesus as a spiritual presence in my heart and soul. Instead, I practiced opening my heart to Buddha – and indeed I found that there were other spiritual presences I could encounter in meditation and trust for guidance, insight, and support.

Then one evening, I was sitting at home alone in my meditation room reading the sayings of Buddha. Quietly, I entered into what is called *Vipassana* meditation, with my full focus on my breathing and my heart. Suddenly, I felt the presence . . . of Jesus inside me.

> At first, I reacted by shutting out Jesus' presence entirely. But as I watched myself doing this, I realized what an utterly foolish thing I was doing. So with a bit of trepidation, I went ahead and risked seeing what would happen if I opened up again to Jesus' direct presence in my life.

Many people, when they break free from the church, do as I did; they cut themselves off from all contact with all things Christian, including the core experience of communing with the spirit of Jesus in their hearts. Why? Probably for fear that they might get sucked back into the whole outdated but somehow-addictive religious thing. But in my case, this wasn't what happened at all. The wonderful feeling now rushing into my heart wasn't linked to Christian belief or dogma or history. What I experienced was primal: that there does exist beyond all religious dogma an expanded dimension of human consciousness where we commune intimately with enlightened spiritual masters of the past who are still alive in spirit in the eternal present moment.

Jesus is surely one of the primary eternal presences that we can tune in to in meditation – or at any time during the day. For our culture, he's the primary link to our essential source. And what is this experience like? Because each new moment is unique, the experience is, of course, always new. But there is for me a special quality when I turn my mind's focus of attention in meditation and prayer toward Jesus' presence.

True spiritual masters are transparent. They're not available to us for ego reasons or earthly emotional games; their spiritual role is to serve as the energetic link between a human soul and God. This, at least, is my experience. And that is how I experience Jesus' presence in meditation.

Because I am mostly a product of my Judeo-Christian upbringing and tradition, it seems natural for me to open up to Jesus' presence within me, and allow his spiritual power to link me with the Ultimate Divine. I can also turn my focus toward other great masters and love comes flowing into my heart. To judge a Buddhist's spiritual experience as less than my own would be folly and unfair. It's very important not to deny the eternal power and presence of other spiritual masters just because they are not the ones who come to you in meditation. In our culture, we turn to Jesus because he's our closest traditional link with the divine. When a Buddhist turns to Buddha, that makes equal sense, doesn't it? There's only one God, after all.

So I reclaimed the baby . . . not by becoming "born again" or rejoining the church, but by having my heart open again to the most direct path I know to eternal love and wisdom.

That's what I mean, plain and simple, by "Jesus without the Church" – putting aside all religious and cultural beliefs that distance us from that primal experience of being heart to heart with Jesus.

This is the most direct way to commune with the infinite presence of God, from which emanates the Holy Spirit that guides our every act in life – if we open up and allow such guidance.

## Believing versus Experiencing

Religious beliefs are curious things. Religion is actually, upon close observation, nothing more than a set of particular beliefs that a group of people over time have decided to hold as sacrosanct and base their lives on. Churches are places where these beliefs are taught, maintained, reinforced, and often forced on members. And what are these beliefs on which religions are built? They're nothing more than *thoughts* – intellectual concepts created and maintained by the logical deductive mental function of the mind.

> Put bluntly, a belief is something we hope is true, even though we don't really know if it's true. When we actually experience something to be true, we no longer need to *believe* it's true – we *know* it is.

I'm in no way denying that traditional Christians sometimes stumble into deep mystical experience and spiritual realization through the priestly path of theological beliefs. Nor am I saying that all or even most priests and ministers, past and present, are conscious of the deviousness and inherent damage potential of the beliefs they press people into believing. All I'm saying is that beliefs don't connect us with God – our direct experience is what brings us to God.

Christians are taught to believe, for instance, that they're born as hopeless sinners. This is a belief – a seriously negative attitude – not a verifiable fact. As another example of a belief, Jesus is reported in the Bible to have been killed and then magically risen from the dead, and in the process to have redeemed our sins, but this again is a hopeful belief, not an experiential fact. In similar mode, believing in an afterlife for true believers is also just that – another belief. We don't know if it's true – we just hope it is.

When I was a youth joining the church, no one talked to me about my ever-changing inner experience of Jesus' guiding presence in my life. All they talked about was what I was supposed to believe – what I had to swear under oath that I believe – which ultimately amounted to nothing more than lofty concepts. After a while, I started to realize that, in this sense, religion and spirituality are polar opposites. At college I read in such books as William James's *The Varieties of Religious Experience* that theology is based on beliefs, which are mental constructs; spirituality, on the other hand, is based on direct inner experience of the truth of life.

> Also, religion is habitually focused on historical events of long ago and on imagined fantasies of an idealized future, whereas spiritual experience is always happening in the eternal here and now.

I will explore these key points in more depth later on in this discussion because they point our attention directly toward our own path to liberation from restricting beliefs, toward an awakening of genuine spiritual experience.

For thousands of years, people have been doing their very best to bring to life what the priests and the Bible tell them they must fervently believe in order to be saved and attain eternal life. Priests likewise have struggled to bring their beliefs and their deeper spiritual experiences into congruence – usually with little success. At the same time, a great many of these people have been having spiritual experiences that reveal a reality quite different from what they have been taught to believe.

> You, of course, have your own unique history related to things religious and spiritual. I've shared some of my experience with you to let you know where I'm coming from. I wonder what your experience over the years has been that would lead you to pick up and start reading this book.

How have you dealt with your own doubts and questions? Have you kept your feelings to yourself, or have you been blessed with good friends with whom you could discuss your deeper spiritual feelings and wonders?

In this book, I'd like to provide you with plenty of open space to pause and reflect on the themes we're exploring. With this in mind, quite often we'll pause at the end of a short discussion to give you time to put the book aside . . . and see what insights, memories, feelings, and other experiences might rise naturally to the surface in this new moment.

Encouraging and exploring these new feelings and insights is probably your primary reason for reading this book. Therefore my intent isn't just to provide you with expanded ideas, but also to encourage your unfolding experience here and now, beyond all ideas.

# ⅍ Pause & Reflect

*If it pleases you, go ahead right now and see what happens if you pause after reading this paragraph, put the book aside, and turn your attention to your inner feelings and spontaneous reflections related to what you've been reading. To do this, just tune in to your breathing . . . open up to the feelings in your heart . . . listen to your quiet inner voice . . . and be open to whatever thoughts, insights, and experiences might come to you . . .*

# ⁂ Pause & Experience

## The Truth Will Set You Free

We all know what a bother it is when one person tries to force another person to believe the same things they believe in. But this is what every child faces from birth – being completely programmed by parents and community to think and behave within a traditional set of core beliefs and values.

Cultures and their accompanying religions are grounded in passing on to the new generation an ancient tradition of what worked in earlier times. This is how human societies survive; the younger generation is programmed with the attitudes and judgments of their elders, so that they carry on with that tried-and-true approach to life. At a certain anthropological level this makes very good sense, because we do benefit greatly from the experience of countless generations before us.

> But especially in these rapidly changing times, I've observed, as a psychologist, that blindly accepting the assumptions, beliefs, and practices of past generations sometimes helps, but can also lead to failure, to personal depression and family tragedy, to economic disaster.

The truth is, the old attitudes and assumptions, especially about how we run our minds and make key decisions, are not serving us very well. Too much of our tradition, even our genetic programming, is fear-based, causing us to react to new situations with outmoded assumptions and defensive actions. Such fear-based and often greed-inducing programming all too often tends toward destruction of the environment, leads to social discord and various forms of violence, and, in general, actually lessens our potential to live fulfilling conscious lives.

> Therefore it seems wise to reflect on the beliefs we've been programmed with, and to let go of those that no longer serve us. With this aim, in this book we'll explore definite ways to learn how to know the truth of the matter directly, through experiencing ourselves what life is all about and then drawing appropriate conclusions.

Specifically related to Christianity, but also in all religions in which a powerful priestly cult has traditionally dominated what people are supposed to believe in their minds and experience in their hearts, it's time to finally say get out of our way. We need no one standing between God and us. When we want help in accessing our Creator, we prefer to turn to the eternal guiding presence of Jesus in our hearts to point us toward the divine. Certainly, the truly spiritual priests and ministers still struggling within the church belief system can help us, but perhaps they first need to see to their own belief structure, before offering help to others.

We'll find in this discussion that when we remove the religious priestly manipulative dimensions that were imbedded in the Gospels, and focus on those sayings of Jesus that ring especially true in our own hearts and souls, we can discover powerful guidelines that help us open up to a new wisdom, and a present-moment spiritual approach to life. In my understanding, the core of what Jesus was teaching – the fulfillment of the prophecies – was that we must learn to let go of the past, move beyond theologies, put aside the priests, and surrender to the direct guidance of our deeper spiritual wisdom. This is how we become truly new creatures upon this Earth – acting powerfully and consistently out of love rather than fear.

> Jesus gave two negative orders in his Gospels: *"Fear not,"* and *"Judge not."* It's time to take these two commandments very seriously, and learn psychologically how to follow his primal recommendations for managing our minds and emotions in this wise direction.

Also, one of the strongest sayings of Jesus that we'll explore in depth is *"Know the truth, and the truth will set you free."* You'll notice he didn't say *think about* the truth or *believe in* the truth. He specifically said, *"Know the truth."* For me, this "knowing" means putting aside assumptions, prejudices, and preprogrammed attitudes and beliefs long enough to experience directly the reality in which we find ourselves living. In this book, we're going to explore the most effective universal meditation process for doing just that.

All cultures evolve as generations come and go. I'd like to share with you my understanding of how our Christian culture is now evolving very rapidly, in so many hearts, into something quite new and deeply hopeful and beautiful. Two thousand years ago, Jesus challenged us to let go of the old and open up to the new – to let go of the priestly cult's fear-based beliefs and promises and, instead, open our hearts directly . . . to experience the love, wisdom, guidance, and power that inflow when we quiet our minds and become one with our Creator.

Let's see how we can use Jesus' teachings as experiential keys to open up to this greater reality. Beyond the limitations of traditional Christianity, in a bright new post-Christian spirit, let's allow Jesus' eternal presence to guide us, support our exploration, and encourage our spiritual awakening and service.

## The New Communion

It seems that in the days right after Jesus' death, the dozen or so dominant men who had followed Jesus took charge. Over several hundred years, a conceptually based theology developed about what Jesus' life had meant, resulting in a written "establishment" belief system to take the place of the oral tradition and living gospel.

> The theologians tried to nail everything down to written statements of belief and theology, rather than holding their focus on the ongoing experience of Jesus in their hearts. And they did all this within the background context of Greek language, Roman religious ambiance, and a general intellectual flourish.

For three hundred years after Jesus died or disappeared, his story and teachings became fragmented into over a hundred differing sects and theologies. Then in the fourth century, a major religious conference was called. The ruling Christian priests and sects dominated the meeting and managed to throw out at least a dozen variant gospels of Jesus' teachings and purpose. They decreed that forevermore, only the four gospels that most supported their own beliefs and rituals would be considered the word of God – and thus was born the New Testament and the Catholic Church.

Twelve hundred bloody years later, after the Inquisition in which the priestly cult of the Catholic Church led a witch hunt that murdered over seven million innocent women in the name of Christ, the newly emerging Protestants rose up against the Catholics and started a new religious movement with a different political structure, but with basically the same theology and male-dominated priestly control. Soon there were major European religious wars being fought and thousands upon thousands more people being killed in the name of Christ.

And today we have new religious wars. Even though Mohammed and Jesus were from the same basic Aramaic bloodline and heritage, even though Mohammed stated clearly that he honored and gave spiritual reverence to Jesus and the Jewish prophets, very soon the Christians were in battle with the Moslems, especially during the Crusades during which Christians attacked Moslems ruthlessly. Many Moslems have not forgotten the Crusades.

> Christianity and Judaism continue to fight Islam. It seems time to open up and allow Spirit in the present moment to guide us. We can accomplish this through a new reading of what Jesus is quoted as saying in the Gospels and a new, more meditative approach to communion with our own deeper spiritual nature . . . and ultimately with God.

Holy Communion in the church – Catholic, Protestant, and independent – has always centered on a reenactment of the Christian version of blood sacrifice. Communion is a ceremony in which true believers prove their faith and dedication to the Christ by ceremonially eating the flesh of his body and drinking his blood. Curiously, this ritual sacrifice is a throwback to much more primitive religious ceremonies hundreds of thousands of years ago, when tribesmen would eat their noble opponents in war in order to ingest and obtain the power and bravery of the person they were eating.

Even when I was quite young, I found Communion's imaginary act of cannibalism grotesque. And when I was kicked out of the church, it was a relief not to push myself through the ceremony ever again. Instead, I began meditating on the word "communion" and what it really means to commune with Jesus' spirit.

> I found that when I steadfastly held my mind's attention on Jesus' spirit in my heart, I experienced my own communion with him and, by direct extension, with God. And while in that state of personal rather than ritualistic communion, insights would come into my heart and mind.

This book is about those insights and also about the meditative process that creates the inner peace and quiet in which communion with Jesus heart to heart is not only possible, but also easy and deeply rewarding.

Let me outline briefly here the flow of our discussions in this book. Please hold in mind throughout that my intent is not to present a new theology, but rather to turn our attention toward new ways of approaching our shared heritage, so that we can let go of existing beliefs and assumptions, free ourselves to experience the deeper truths of our tradition, and commune with the still-living presence, power, and guidance of this spiritual being called Jesus.

## Part One: Discovering the New Jesus

This first section of our discussion explores seven crucial choices that determine how we approach our spiritual heritage and experience Jesus' presence in our lives. In each chapter, I'll show you how the church has tended to direct our *minds* in making these key choices, and then offer alternative choices, which are fully supported by what Jesus said in the Gospels. This section creates time and space for a beginning reflective process wherein I offer you alternate spiritual paths, and then let you choose for yourself.

> You'll find that as long as you habitually fix your attention on limiting theological beliefs, you are not free to open up and experience directly the greater truth of the matter.

This is why we need to evaluate consciously our existing beliefs and then choose to put some of them aside if we find that they stand between God and us.

## Part Two: Living the New Relationship

Seven key sayings of Jesus have for many years rung so loud, clear, and true in my life and meditations that they have become the foundation of my meditations when I turn my mind's attention toward Jesus. The seven short chapters in this section delve into each of these sayings in turn, providing you with a solid set of phrases from Jesus that will act to turn your mind's attention directly where he seems to have most strongly recommended. These commandments come from the heart, resonate throughout the soul, and guide us toward direct encounter with our divine wisdom and awakening.

## Part Three: Experiencing the New Meditation

By this point in the book, we're ready to move into the actual meditation process that emerges naturally from what we've explored thus far from Jesus' primary meditative sayings. I use the word "meditation" here in the secular, nonesoteric sense of the word: quieting the mind and opening our hearts to directly encounter and experience divine light and wisdom and the inflow of God's presence into our personal consciousness.

This is a new form of prayer, not based on ideas, theology, and beliefs, but on opening the heart, mind, and soul to the actual heart-to-heart feeling of being in deep communion with God.

## Extra Help and Guidance

I hope you find the discussions and new meditation process in this book deeply rewarding. To help you learn this meditation by heart, feel free also to go to www.johnselby.com where you can listen to streamed-audio programs with my voice guiding you through the meditation process. You'll find several variations, depending on how much time you have available, plus an extended online course and a forum where you can ask me any questions that might be on your mind about this process.

Words help point your attention in rewarding directions. But the wise teacher knows when to be silent and step aside so that you are completely free to commune in your own way with your deeper spiritual reality. When you read the last page of this book, you will be ready to act on your own as you explore a lifelong communion and journey with your Creator. I thank you for trusting me to be your guide in approaching this ultimate experience. May you experience continual lifelong blessings on your journey to your source!

## Reflection Time

*You might want to pause now, put the book aside . . . tune in to your breathing . . . and your heart . . . and reflect on what we've talked about thus far. What are your feelings about all this? Is this blasphemy to be avoided, or liberation to be actively encouraged inside your own heart?*

 Pause & Reflect

**Part One**

# Discovering the New Jesus

In this first section, we're going to explore what happens when we stop holding ingrained religious *concepts and old-time attitudes about* Jesus and God, and instead turn our mind's attention toward the *direct experience* of God's presence and wisdom – right here in this present moment.

> There are seven primary choices to reflect on if you desire to let go of cultural programming and discover the reality of your relationship with Jesus and God in the present moment. These first chapters provide an examination of those choices.

This first section, written in a somewhat provocative tone, challenges you to consider the possibility that a number of church doctrines run contrary to psychological logic and are downright unhealthy. In parts 2 and 3, we'll explore the actual reflective process based on Jesus' meditative teachings, which will enable you to "know the truth" that will set you free.

# 1

# From Christ . . . to Jesus

The very first choice we're going to explore is also perhaps the most challenging for those of you who, as children, imprinted strongly on traditional Christian beliefs and dogma. Given the choice, do you want to spend your spiritual life focusing on the theological concept of the Christ as a symbolic *belief* in your mind, or on the actual *experience* of Jesus as a living spiritual presence in your heart?

Psychologists have found that you can't hold your focus of attention at the same time on *an idea or thought* (a past-future function of your mind) and *an experience* (a present-moment function of your mind). You must choose between beliefs (ideas) and actual inner experiences. Christian beliefs often run contrary to the spiritual experiences that come to us when we focus on our deeper intuitive and mystical realms of being. So, yes, we must choose between holding on to our cherished beliefs about the Christ and letting go of those beliefs in order to fully embrace Jesus in our hearts.

If you're like most people in our culture, you naturally absorbed many images, ideas, and assumptions about Jesus while you were growing up. You probably have a general if somewhat vague sense of his life as a historical figure. You might remember sayings he's supposed to have uttered. You perhaps hold an image of his face, or his body on the cross, taken from drawings and paintings you've seen. And these days, you might have had movie images fried into your brain from a recent almost pornographically violent movie rendition of this man's life and passion.

> In our spiritual lives, do these images and imaginings help us encounter the living presence of Jesus in our hearts? My experience has been that all such fantasies about Jesus stand in our way of actually opening our hearts to feel and experience his presence directly.

As you progress through this book, I hope you'll come to see your existing images for what they are – second-hand programming – and begin to shift your attention away from fantasies toward your present-moment experiential connection with what lies beyond the images.

Most of us also have quite an assortment of ideas and concepts, beliefs and philosophies about Jesus not as a spiritual person but as an ideal religious concept called the Christ. These ideas and beliefs likewise can serve to distance you from the actual experience of Jesus' spirit in your life. Quotes from the Gospels can be separated into two distinct groups: those sayings that feel like they come from the human Jesus speaking heart to heart, and those that seem to come from a symbolic ideal Christ, aimed at establishing theological doctrine and religious dogma.

> When you focus your mind's attention on Jesus, you'll find that you focus on a vital heart-to-heart experience that is felt in the present moment, right now. When you focus on

the Christ, you'll notice that you shift away from experience into the thinking mode of consciousness, as you fixate on religious thoughts that often exist without any feelings or heart engagement at all.

As you'll see especially in the final meditation section of this book, choosing where you aim your mind's attention – toward "experience" or "concept," toward Jesus or the Christ – strongly determines the type of spiritual experience that comes to you, or doesn't. Ultimately, you need to make that choice. Choosing to focus on *concepts* enables you to remain in the traditional Christian world. Choosing to focus on inspired spiritual *experience* shifts you into the new era of Jesus, called post-Christian living. Please don't think you have to make the choice now – we're just beginning our exploration.

## Finding Jesus – Really

Jesus does seem to have been a historical person who lived and taught and loved and died and who knows what else around two thousand years ago in and around Jerusalem. His eternal spiritual presence ever since has permeated human hearts and souls who have opened to direct communion with him at deep spiritual dimensions of consciousness.

As you probably know, very little can be verified about Jesus the historical man. We know that he did exist and that he appeared before the authorities, but that's about all the mention we can find anywhere outside the Bible. He was a young Jewish man who developed a large following and then was executed, as were hundreds of other young Jewish men in and around Jerusalem two thousand years ago – many of them for leading insurrections and claiming to be the great leader or Messiah who would finally rid Israel of the armies from Rome.

The next fact we know historically is that ten to 20 years after Jesus was killed or otherwise disappeared, various religious groups claiming Jesus as their lord and savior were springing into existence. They got into trouble with the authorities and were therefore mentioned more and more frequently in Greek and Roman historical accounts. It does appear that the historical Jesus was a man who had a radical impact on those who followed him.

> He was also a leader whose presence, one way or another, continued to be felt not only by his direct followers, but also by others who learned of his life and teachings and could feel his presence in their own hearts even decades after his death.

Definitely, something of a deep spiritual quality continued after Jesus the man died, and this ongoing spiritual presence continued to touch the hearts and lives of so many that new theologies, communities, and conflicts began to take root, never to be permanently suppressed.

In the next few generations, various written accounts appeared, more than 20 in all that we know of, called the Gospels of Jesus Christ. From these writings, we know a bit of the historical Jesus. And from our own hearts and souls, we know of the spiritual presence that continues. If you haven't felt this direct inner encounter with Jesus in your heart, the meditations at the end of this book will provide you with the opportunity.

Please don't think that this book or meditation method is "pushing Jesus" in any way. I am not a Jesus freak and I do not feel any need to push other people in the direction I am exploring. We all have our paths to explore spiritually. I'm writing this book with zero pressure for those of you who for one reason or another feel an inclination to turn your meditative attention toward the presence that is most commonly called Jesus.

## Behold the Christ

Now we come to something entirely different from the historical and spiritual Jesus: the term I finally had to let go in order to embrace my deeper spiritual experience. Jesus almost certainly was *not* called the Christ when he was walking this earth. The term "Christ" didn't even exist in the language Jesus spoke. It's a lofty Greek religious concept, which evolved directly from the more ancient Hindu concept of Krishna in the Sanskrit language of India. In both of these religious traditions, there developed the idea of a god who came to earth to save us from our inherent animal nature and raise us up into a higher spiritual level of existence. Only after Jesus died did people begin to start to think that perhaps Jesus was the Christ.

When I was at seminary, I studied the four Gospels in depth, looking for final certainty about who Jesus was, and whether he was the Christ or simply had that radical title attached to his memory after he was gone. But the deeper I looked into the Bible, the less I found there of rock-solid veracity.

> It's important to note in this context that not a single word that Jesus spoke in his indigenous dialect of Aramaic was written down, at least to the knowledge of biblical scholars. At first, the words that Jesus spoke were passed down only by word of mouth, until someone started gathering these sayings and wrote them down – in Greek.

The first gospel in the Bible to be written down, at least as far as we know, was the Gospel of Mark, usually dated as being penned around 60 to 70 years after Jesus died. Please note that the term "Christian" is never mentioned in this gospel. And only four times in total does the term "Christ" appear, each time very obviously pushing one of Mark's key theological points. Usually, Jesus was referred to instead as the Messiah. This was a genuine Hebrew term quite different from the Greek term "Christ," in that the Jews in Israel anticipated a historical savior who would liberate them from the occupying military forces from Rome.

When crowds shouted to Jesus that he was the Messiah, they most certainly weren't talking about a foreign philosophical concept; they were referring to this very physical human being who was going to lead them into victory against the Romans. But 60 years later, when the story of Jesus was finally written down, in Greek, the term *Messiah* was cleverly translated as "Christ."

By the time the Gospel of Mark was finally written down, numerous Jesus sects had come into being – each with its own distinct theological opinion about who Jesus was and what his life and resurrection from the dead meant symbolically, from a religious point of view. Let me share with you just one short passage from a very early letter written about the development of Mark's gospel, so you can see how the texts we tend to regard as sacrosanct were actually, from the beginning, being written to push a particular religious party line.

Below is part of a letter by Clement of Alexandria "to Theodore" regarding the origins of the Gospel of Mark. The ancient letter was discovered by Morton Smith in 1958 when he, as a graduate student of Columbia University, was cataloguing the manuscript collection of the Mar Saba Monastery south of Jerusalem:

> As for Mark, during the time when Peter was in Rome, he wrote up the deeds of the Lord, not actually recording everything, nor hinting at the mysteries, but instead picking out the things he thought would increase the faith of those being taught. From the things he remembered hearing from Peter, he supplemented his book with the appropriate items. He did not reveal the things which are not to be discussed. He added certain sayings which he knew would initiate the hearers into the innermost sanctuary of the truth.

As noted, even in this first gospel of Jesus' teachings, there is admittedly much left out and considerable manipulation of the text for the specific goal of teaching believers a particular theology. For me, the key words in this early letter about Jesus' recorded sayings are the following: "*He added certain sayings which he knew would initiate the hearers into the innermost sanctuary of the truth . . .* " Which sayings in Mark are these "certain sayings" of Jesus? These are the particular quotes I've done my best to identify in the Gospels that seem most powerful in providing direct access to Jesus as a spiritual conduit into "the innermost sanctuary of the truth."

## Selling the Christ

The Gospels written first historically have the fewest mentions of the Christ. The final gospel, John, has the most. The term arises only four times in Mark, and 20 times in John. Rather than focusing on the abstract symbolic Christ, the four books telling the story of Jesus are mostly focused on Jesus not as a symbolic religious archetype, but as a human teacher who told stories about how best to lead our lives.

Jesus really only became the Christ in his death and resurrection – that's when he "proved" his mystical worth and became the core symbol of Christianity. That's when he moved from a heart experience to a heady idea. When I was at seminary, I had to read volume after volume of theological writings arguing about the meaning of the term "Christ" and what I'm supposed to teach people in my congregation to believe in this regard.

But even in the Bible, the entire account of Jesus rising from the dead is mentioned only in several very short, questionable accounts. Of the entire New Testament, less than one page actually describes the core resurrection event and Jesus' transcendent physical appearances after his crucifixion. It's truly amazing that the entire Christian belief system and church are built on such scant accounts.

Jesus was a person who seems to have attained enlightenment and who continues as a spiritual presence to touch our hearts and guide our deeper lives. But Christ as a concept is something altogether different. The Christ is a radically large and powerful concept, because within the concept are the belief and promise that Jesus became the Christ and therein became symbolic as a personal savior sent by God to forever free true believers from their hopelessly sinful natures and enable them to live forever and ever, amen.

> That's a giant promise – ultimate liberation from death, eternal freedom from mortality, total protection from evil forces, secure escape from the obliteration of our ego personalities and maybe even our physical bodies . . .

Along with such a promise, however, comes a certain ultimate requirement. You must surrender your soul to that belief system. You must bow down to Christ as your Lord and agree to accept all the theological dogma that accompanies the promise. In Christian theology, there's no middle ground. You're either for Christ or against him. From the earliest beginnings of the church, its priests have posited this radical conflict-generating duality. If you don't choose to join their organization and follow their dictums, then you automatically become the enemy. Not only that, you are also condemned to eternal damnation and hellfire.

When one steps back and asks dispassionately why Christianity has become such a powerful force in human history, it's all too easy to answer the question with a negative twist. Christianity has been so successful in recruiting members to its organization because it happens to have the best sales pitch in history – except perhaps for the Moslems, who also throw in 90 virgins when you get to heaven.

In the Christian deal, if only you can talk yourself into believing that you are a hopeless sinner and that some wonderful human being who was half god suffered terribly and died because of you, then, by your act of accepting this whole scenario, you will never have to face the obliteration of your ego.

> Everyone's afraid to die, and if you accept the theological dogma of the Christian priests, you sidestep the entire issue of death. Instead you settle into the belief that your personal ego presence is going to go to heaven – where life is eternal and perfect and you can live forever.

There are, of course, other attached beliefs that you also have to talk yourself into – that Jesus the Christ was conceived through God himself somehow coming down to earth and engaging in sexual intercourse with a Jewish girl named Mary, thus creating a unique half-God, half-human being. You must believe that God Almighty has a male personality and is engaged in celestial battle with one of his fallen angels called Satan – who can grab your soul and send you to eternal hellfire if you're not very careful about what you believe and what experiences you allow to come into your mind and heart.

Furthermore, to be a Christian, you need to talk yourself into believing that something that happened two thousand years ago in a culture entirely different from your own directly determines your present-moment fate. You must base your current religious life on just one historical document called the Bible and, in so doing, you must take on the religious heritage of a distant Arab tribe because their Old Testament is considered the Word of God. You must believe that every word written in the Bible is the holy Word of God, and not in any way influenced by the personal beliefs, quirks, and power plays of that book's multitude of historical writers and editors.

If you can manage to swallow all that doctrine (and considerably more), then and only then do you get forgiveness for your sinful nature, special access to the love of Jesus the Christ, communion with your Creator, and a salvation that includes liberation from death itself.

Unfortunately, there's always the lingering doubt in every believer's mind that maybe there isn't really any heaven to go to, maybe when death comes, that's the end. Even more frightening is the fear that your faith isn't strong enough, that the doubts that attack you might overcome you, and then as you fall from grace, the Devil himself will be right there to grab your soul and drop you into the boiling cauldron of Hell forevermore.

That's the ongoing priestly sales pitch that has grown up around Jesus' original teachings and ongoing spiritual presence. That was what I as a minister was supposed to sell and, having been brought up in that faith, I did give it a try. But as I matured and began to explore my own spiritual experience, I found that it all started to make less and less sense to me. My inner experience of Jesus in my heart and soul simply didn't have anything to do with the beliefs about Christ.

> Christianity is built on our all-too-human fears of death – and on the priestly promise of escaping death through accepting and supporting (even violently) that particular intellectual belief system.

I am in no way saying there is no afterlife. I have a strong hunch that there is life of some sort beyond death. I'm only saying that it's a dirty trick to lure people into your church by pretending that your particular church holds the only key to eternity.

## Jesus Himself

Jesus the person does seem to have been a fully realized spiritual human being, a man who somehow discovered and fully entered into his true spiritual nature and oneness with God, and then encouraged his followers to do the same by following his path of the heart. This human being died and entered a nonphysical, spiritual realm where his presence can still be experienced directly.

My experience is that, without entering into any contract to believe any dogma about the meaning of Jesus' life and death, we can learn simple meditation methods that help open our hearts so we can encounter this spiritual presence in our personal consciousness. Through opening to the power of Jesus' love, we can discover and awaken our own eternal oneness with God.

> This is the heart path that Jesus discovered and taught. And you don't have to sell your soul to join the club – all you have to do is open your heart to the inflow of Spirit and surrender to God's guidance in your life.

This experiential approach (feeling, not thought) to Jesus isn't grounded at all in the past. You don't have to believe one way or the other about what happened two thousand years ago. And there is no future dimension to a meditative approach to Jesus – because when you live in the eternal present moment, you realize directly that this is it, that life is eternal, and that rather than being a hopeless sinner, you're born perfect.

You do have the moment-to-moment choice of focusing on this experiential Jesus, or going in the opposite direction and focusing on the symbol, belief, and concept of the Christ. There's certainly a strong pull to live in beliefs rather than direct experience. Concepts and beliefs, as long as we can accept them and hold on to them, offer a certainty and finality that are very alluring. Abstractions stand outside chronological time; therefore they have a sense of permanence that can seem very worthwhile to maintain.

But there's such a major downside! When you live mostly in beliefs, as Christians are supposed to, you're mostly lost in your head somewhere. You're not plugged experientially into the real pulse of life. You're missing out on the action in the present moment, where life actually takes place.

Beliefs are totally grounded in the past. Experience is grounded in the eternal now, which is alive with the power of love and Jesus' infinite presence. You can't be in the past and the present moment at the same time. You've got to choose where you're going to place your bet. The Christ is an abstract idea. Jesus is a living reality. Which do you prefer?

Obviously, I have chosen experience over concept, the present moment over the past and future. I've let go of the Christ because I'd rather *feel* Jesus in my heart as my guiding light than *think about* and *believe in* Christ in my head. The rewards in my spiritual life have been truly wonderful, and there has been no downside. The priests and ministers tell you to choose in one direction. I'm suggesting that you'll thrive spiritually by choosing the opposite direction. And lightning hasn't struck me yet!

> But you and you alone must look and see which choice means most to you, what works for you – and live your life accordingly. This book is designed to help you experience for yourself what is most important and real in your life.

If you happen to be a fervent traditional Christian believer and have read this far into this book, perhaps you're ready to shout "blasphemy!" All I ask is that you look at the same truth I'm looking at, and see what you see. Yes, I am indeed thinking and acting outside the traditional Christian box. Luckily, we live in a period of history where we're not in danger of being burned at the stake, as would have happened if I'd written this book five hundred years ago. We are making progress.

# ⚘ Reflection Time

Take time to relax and put this book aside, so you can reflect on your feelings and thoughts related to this somewhat provocative discussion. I certainly don't expect you to see all this exactly as I do. I'm simply sharing with you the process that I've gone through, in shifting from head-tripping about Christ and salvation to a more heart-centered approach to life.

My intent is to point your almighty power of attention in directions that can bring you into direct encounter with your own experience of Jesus in your life . . . and then to get out of your way as you discover what's real in all this.

So feel free to take time now to reflect on how you feel about what you've been reading . . . allow your attention to tune in to your own breathing . . . be aware of, and accept, the feelings in your heart . . . and see what insights come . . . as you reflect on living your life either immersed in thoughts and beliefs about the Christ or experiencing Jesus' actual presence in your heart and soul . . . and throughout, stay aware of your breathing to hold you in the here and now, and, as always, be open to a new experience!

# ⚘ Pause & Experience

# 2

# From Intellect . . . to the Heart

Compared with other creatures on this planet, we human beings are champs when it comes to the intellect. Each of us is born with an amazing brain that gives us almost miraculous potential for exploring the outer world and our inner experiences – and also for reflecting on these experiences. Not only can we be aware of all the sensory input that bombards our minds moment to moment, we can also think about, remember, and reflect on what we encounter, so that we become aware of our own presence in the world. This seemingly unique human capacity for reflective self-consciousness is what makes spiritual experience possible.

As I've discussed in various books, you yourself possess a sum total of not just one but six distinct mental functions, all working together (or sometimes at odds with each other) to generate your moment-to-moment experience.

1. Thinking: Right now you're using your cognitive intellectual function to process and make sense of the words you're reading.

2. Memory/Imagination: If my words stimulate images or experiences from your past, or imaginings of any kind, you're using a second valuable function of your brain that stores the past as memory.

3. Emotions: If my words evoke emotions or mood shifts in your body, you're tapping into that vast realm of emotional response orchestrated by yet another distinct brain function.

4. Perceptions: If you're aware of any sensory experiences – sounds, skin sensations, smells, or whatever – happening as you read these words, you're tapping your mind's perceptual function.

These are the four mental functions people usually focus on in their lives – the basic functions that support survival in everyday life. But you have two other key ways of using your mind that are often overlooked and undernourished but that truly make you human and whole – and raise your quality of consciousness into spiritual realms.

5. Intuition: This is your capacity to shift from focusing your attention on a point (logical deductive reasoning and perception) to "seeing everything at once," perceiving the whole. This is when you suddenly enjoy a flash of realization or creativity in which you see the world in a new way and realize a more creative approach to your situation. This is also the level of consciousness where spiritual insights can begin to rise to the surface.

6. Meditation: Your highest mental function is that of deep reflection, contemplation, and meditation. Many people barely use this capacity at all because they are so locked in their more mundane mental buzz that they don't know how to shift into this truly spiritual state of mind. In this expanded quality of consciousness, everyday thoughts become quiet, worries are put aside, inner peace and a sense of connectedness with your source are felt – and spiritual wisdom, love, insight, and guidance are free to flow into your heart.

We do best when we nurture all six functions of the mind. It's wonderful, fun, and essential for our survival to spend considerable time thinking, planning, problem-solving, and otherwise locked into cognitive reasoning gear. It's also important and a pleasure to take time to remember happenings and people from past experience, and to drift into daydreams and imaginings about the future. Likewise it's key to stay in touch with our emotions and the deeper feelings in our hearts. Present-moment awareness of our sensory experience is absolutely essential, as is regularly tuning in to our intuitive creative experience.

And, although this fact is often overlooked, regular time needs to be devoted to quieting the mind, calming the emotions, and letting go of the past and the future, so that in reflection and meditation we contact deeper wisdom, inspiration, and guidance, and maintain our inner lives immersed in spiritual realms.

## The Phenomenon Called Spirit

What do I mean when I speak of "spiritual realms" and the presence of Spirit in our lives? The born-again movement has so overused and misused the term "spirit" that I often find it hard even to use the word. But I do feel that it's important to reclaim this term because, well – there's just no word that can take its place.

I'd like to share with you my understanding and experience regarding the reality to which the term "spirit" symbolically points. All words, of course, are symbols that point our attention toward something. The term "spirit" has been used throughout the world for many thousands of years to point attention toward a wide variety of experiences, and a wide variety of assumptions and beliefs based at least partially on those experiences.

In ancient tribal traditions, people claimed to experience spirits associated with almost everything in their world. Based on tribal folklore and priestly belief systems, there were tree spirits and deer spirits and water spirits and wind spirits – the whole universe was populated and controlled by a spirit world back in ancient days. These spirits interacted with human beings, sometimes cooperating, sometimes causing problems for the tribe. To further complicate the situation, witch doctors and shamans claimed to have the power to influence the spirits to do good, or perhaps to harm someone.

**From very early times, the priestly cult in all tribes seems to have ruled the minds and hearts of the community by using fear of spiritual danger to manipulate people's beliefs and behavior.**

I'm not here to cast judgment on the relative validity or superstitious nature of early religious beliefs about the spiritual world, but I do, I admit, tend to be bothered by the priestly cult's tendency to employ fear-based manipulations to control the minds and hearts of the populace.

Around seven to ten thousand years ago, the ruling priestly cults in many major societies began to believe in (and, it is to be hoped, experience) a higher order of spirit participation in the universe. These spirits were labeled "gods." By the time Jesus was born, many societies around the world had evolved to where they believed in a pantheon of higher-order gods – the sun god, the moon god, a god who controlled the wind, a god who controlled fertility, and all the rest. Along with the gods came a new order of religious leaders who claimed to have power to interact with and influence these higher-order gods.

These gods were said to live in the heavens above, not on Earth. But each god was said to have its own individual spirit, and this spirit had powers to move invisibly here on Earth and influence the physical world. Through such invisible spirit movement and action, each god could touch a human being's heart and mind, as well as impact events of the physical world. Not only in Greece, Rome, and Egypt, but also in India, China, the Americas, and elsewhere, these gods (and their related priests) ruled the human populace for thousands of years.

There were a few nice gods, but there were also quite a few

seriously mean gods. In general, people seemed to have been much more afraid of the spirit world than they were soothed by it.

But regardless of variations in beliefs about the spirit world, almost all human traditions were aware of something happening at the nonphysical spiritual level of consciousness. Beyond three-dimensional phenomena, most people believed in, and experienced, a deeper realm of life that remained mysterious but important in the minds and souls of the populace.

Then something quite new began to emerge, especially in the Near East among certain Arab tribes. One of these tribes, called the Israelites, began to evolve a tradition that believed in and experienced not a bunch of spirits or a pack of gods, but one ultimate infinite God the Creator. This infinite presence in heaven came and touched the world and human hearts through his Holy Spirit, often in the physical appearance of heavenly angels.

As the concept and experience of this God Almighty advanced and evolved with the passing of the centuries, this originally quite wrathful God came to be experienced more and more as a loving God. Its compassionate spirit often reached out and touched people's hearts and, in the process, connected them through love with the source of all creation.

Of course, from a more dispassionate perspective, almost certainly it wasn't God who was changing over the centuries, becoming less wrathful and more compassionate. My understanding is that the spiritual reality of the universe hasn't been changing. What's been changing has been our human capacity to tune in to and experience this spiritual reality on deeper and deeper levels.

Limited human beliefs about God directly, and sadly, restrict our ability to encounter God. And, equally sadly, the priestly cults throughout the world seem to have quite purposefully taught fear-based beliefs about God in order to manipulate and rule with a heavy hand.

But in every culture, the more enlightened priests certainly struggled to expand the beliefs of the populace, so that a more intimate and loving relationship could develop between human beings and their Creator. I tend to be a little harsh on the priests of ancient days because there is strong evidence that they put more fear than love into the hearts of their brethren. A quick look at Christian history shows just how deadly religious rulers can become when they succumb to the lure of absolute power and seemingly God-ordained dominion, rather than focusing on their hearts and the love that ultimately sustains the true spiritual world. But always there were true spiritual seekers among the priestly caste, who struggled to awaken to a higher communion with Spirit and to expand their religious tradition in more loving directions. The same is certainly true today.

Finally, in the history of the Jewish tribe, along came Jesus. Here was a man who somehow became conscious at a new level, who was somehow in touch with God his Creator at a new depth and in relationship with his fellow human beings in a new way.

We have no idea how Jesus attained his enlightened state of mind. But when he was ready, he spent the final few years of his life trying to share his spiritual insights and vision with his friends and followers. The four Gospels give us a tiny fragment of the nature and success of his teaching phase.

In my humble opinion, based on the evidence in the Gospels, Jesus wasn't all that successful as a mass-audience teacher. Most of the people who started following and worshipping him didn't seem to "get" what he was talking about. He was teaching a new way of relating with God, but they were hearing what he was saying with ears that could not hear. Their prevailing beliefs and attitudes kept them from opening up and tuning in to what he had discovered.

Often Jesus is reported to have become frustrated, exhorting his followers to wake up, but not seeming to have much success in that attempt. He was teaching a subtle inward path and they were locked into old attitudes and expectations. They wanted a leader who would chase the Romans out of their country. What they got instead was a tragedy in which a quiet, peaceful spiritual teacher ended up being caught in violent political games and killed.

## Jesus' True Power

My experience is that Jesus' impact on the world – and it has been gigantic – has not come primarily from his written teachings or the theologies that developed about and around his teachings. The touch of Jesus' love and guidance has not been passed around primarily through actions and sermons of the priests and ministers. Rather, Jesus' touch, love, and guidance have been received by literally billions of human beings through the *presence* of his spirit, through the *inflow* of the Holy Spirit into people's hearts.

Spirit is most certainly still alive, active, and vital in the world today, just as it was in Jesus' day (and for all of time). Spirit, after all, in its pure true form, is God's eternal presence in the world. How it manifests in people's lives depends on the consciousness of each person receiving (or denying) it.

> Spirit does not push into our lives. It doesn't force changes in our beliefs, attitudes, and religious dogma. Spirit, in my experience, is a pure clean infinite loving wisdom and presence that come flowing into our hearts to the extent and in the format we allow.

What's most important here is the fact that *Spirit is not an idea*. Spirit is not a theological concept. Spirit is not a belief. Spirit is *real* – it's a power, a presence, a wisdom, and a guiding force that comes flowing into our hearts, if only we let it.

Many people try to use their thoughts to open up to God, but Spirit simply doesn't enter through the intellectual function of our minds. Why? Because thinking is a past-future process of the mind. We get "lost in thought" – we're absent from the present moment, where Spirit is felt – when we're thinking.

All human experience happens in the here and now, not in the past or the future. Experience is purely present-oriented. And the experience of Spirit in our lives is just that, an experience. We feel the presence of God in our hearts. Certainly, when we allow Spirit to fill our hearts, our thinking is influenced by this experience. But it is important to realize that, spiritually, our heart is our center. God is love. Spirit inflows through our heart and then radiates throughout our being.

> More and more psychologists agree with the ancient spiritual masters that experientially there is no past, there is no future – there is only the eternal here and now. So only when we have our minds' focus on the here and now can Spirit actually touch our lives.

Touch, after all, is a sensation; it's something we feel. It's an experience, plain and simple. And when we're thinking, out of touch with our present-moment feelings, we're actually shutting Spirit out of our lives. That's why, in all meditation traditions, learning how to shift out of thinking into present-moment experiencing is absolutely vital.

## The Heart Path

Jesus, as we'll see, very much taught this same lesson: that the kingdom of heaven is at hand, here in the eternal present moment. Furthermore this kingdom of heaven can only be entered when the thinking mind is quieted and our focus of attention is turned to our hearts. Jesus' primary message was that love is the central quality of a spiritual life. And love is a feeling in the heart. Like Spirit, love is an experience. Yes, we can reflect on love and even get totally lost in thoughts about love. But to experience love, we must quiet our minds and tune in to our hearts.

> In all the world's great meditative traditions, including the contemplative Christian traditions, there is only one path to spiritual awakening, and that is the path of the heart, the path of love, the path of present-moment encounter with Spirit not as an abstract thought in the head, but as a very real feeling in the heart.

Please don't get me wrong here. I personally am a great lover of abstract thought. I love to think, as do we all except when we get stuck in fear-based worries. But I have also learned that it's vital to manage my mind so that my thoughts don't dominate my life.

## Post-Christian Faith

In traditional Christian worship, we *think about* and *imagine* and *talk about* God. In post-Christian practice, the emphasis is on quieting the mind entirely, and *listening* to God. In church dogma, faith focuses on trusting our beliefs to be true. In the approach I'm recommending, faith focuses on trusting our experiences of spiritual encounter and realization. The shift is from nonstop cognitive activity, to sustained experiential encounter with the divine.

In this light, a great deal of my professional life has been spent exploring how we can quiet our minds and turn our attention toward our heart experience. I welcome you to go to my website if you want to read in more detail about the research and techniques that have emerged from this lifelong study. Most people do not have control of their own minds. Thoughts stream endlessly through the mind, and the inner ego voice constantly talks away, maintaining a nonstop judgmental narrative on everything that's happening. You surely know this stream-of-consciousness function of your mind.

Unfortunately, most of us take our talk-talk function of the mind with us even when we enter into prayer and meditation. We talk to God, rather than being quiet so we can hear what God might have to say to us. And the bottom line is this: As long as we're thinking, as long as we're caught up in our own ideas, attitudes, and busyness in the head, we are shut off from any heart-to-heart communion with God. Until we learn to quiet our minds, we're mostly separate from our own spiritual presence. Sad, but true.

In the Old Testament, you will find eight words said to be the words of God himself: "Be still – and know that I am God." There's the primal order – to quiet our minds. Because only when we do this are we receptive to knowing directly, in our hearts, the presence of God in our lives.

And this "knowing" that happens when our thoughts are quiet is an experience that happens in our hearts. Over and over, Jesus told his followers to put aside their worried thoughts, their scheming about the future, and their judgments about the past. He told them to stop judging altogether, stop worrying too – and these are both functions of the thinking mind.

In this light, when I suggest that you quiet your mind, tune in to the present moment, and open your heart to Jesus and the Holy Spirit, I'm suggesting that without any beliefs or other cultural filters through which you judge, limit, and define Spirit, you go ahead and open up – simply surrender to the inflow of God's presence in your life.

For me this is the true post-Christian act of faith: to trust that when you silence your thinking mind and turn your mind's attention to the eternal presence of Jesus, you will receive the pure touch of spiritual guidance and love of God in your life.

Again – this is an *experience, not a thought.* And it happens in your heart, not in your head. And it's always awaiting you, to the extent that you, at least momentarily, put aside your beliefs and welcome

25

pure Spirit into your heart – without any preconditioned expectations at all.

## The Transformer

To end this chapter, I'd like to introduce a new, science-friendly metaphor concerning how Jesus' presence fits naturally into the experience of opening to God's love, touch, and guidance. At first, this metaphor might seem a bit unusual, but as we progress you'll probably find that the metaphor closely reflects what actually happens in your experience when you open to Jesus' presence in your heart.

First, let's ask scary but essential questions: Why do we need Jesus in the meditation equation at all? Why include his spiritual presence in our relationship with God? For a number of years after leaving my work in the church, I seriously asked myself this same question. After all, I could learn how to meditate, I could learn how to quiet my thoughts, and I could (sometimes) open up to God's love and guidance – all without Jesus. Without Jesus, was something missing?

In short form, here's what I've come to understand about the vital role of enlightened beings in the spiritual experience of everyday human beings. Please remember that I'm not asking you to accept everything I'm saying here. I'm simply sharing my experience for what it's worth. Here are the metaphor and the underlying spiritual process that make great sense to me.

The power and effect of the electricity that our modern civilization is built on are sent to our community from its generation source via great power lines that carry immense energy. This massive powerhouse of energy poses a practical problem: If an individual home wants to tap into this power, the energy is simply too great. Rather than empowering the house, the surge of such an immense charge would ignite and destroy the house with its vastly superior power. Therefore, between the main source of power and the individual user, there must be placed a transformer that "drops the charge of energy down" to a greatly reduced charge that the individual house can absorb and use, rather than be over-whelmed by.

> My experience is that, in much the same way, most of us most of the time seem to need a spiritual "transformer" between us and the radical power and glory of God Almighty. The intermediary presence of enlightened beings such as Jesus (and in other traditions, Buddha, Lao Tzu, and so on) somehow fulfills this transformer role in our lives.

Because Jesus' presence seems to be grounded both in earthly mortality and transcendent divinity, he can serve as the needed transformer when we turn our attention toward the infinite power of the divine. This is my deeper understanding of the otherwise rather priestly statement attributed to Jesus, "No one comes to the Father but through me." We do need (at least sometimes) to include Jesus in our spiritual-communion equation.

Does this mean that we will get zapped and obliterated if we turn our mind's meditative focus directly toward God without Jesus' loving presence between us? No, certainly not. We seem to have our own inner transformer that enables us to focus on the infinite divine directly. You can turn your attention to your heart, quiet your mind, and open to Spirit and, always, a unique experience will come to you. You are quite capable of tuning directly in to the presence of your Creator with no one – not even a Savior – between you and your Maker.

Here's what I have discovered that has made all the difference in my life, however. In meditation or prayer (they're mostly one and the same once you quiet your mind), the experience I am able to receive is qualitatively different when I include Jesus' spiritual presence in the equation.

> I sometimes have no desire or need to focus my attention on Jesus' presence. But often when I enter into meditation, I experience a natural hunger in my heart to open up to Jesus' presence first, so that I can then receive the unique

divine encounter that I can only express as "God coming to me through Jesus."

So there you have it, a new notion regarding why we need Jesus in our spiritual lives – not as a Savior for our sinful nature, not as a safe pass to avoid mortal death, but as a spiritual transformer that enables us to experience the infinite divine in a unique way. I have difficulty expressing this ultimately deep notion in words – I hope you get the general idea, and will explore step by step the reality beyond these words.

## Reflection Time

*I wonder what you're thinking about all this. I encourage you to observe regularly your mind's various reactions to my words, and also notice how your heart is responding to what I'm suggesting. In this spirit, let's take a break so that you can pause, shift your mind's attention down to your heart . . . and observe whatever feelings you find there.*

*That's the primal act we're encouraging – shifting your mind's attention to your heart. Yes, sometimes you'll find pain when you look there, sometimes anxiety, sometimes any number of emotions. Often you might just find numbness. Throughout this book, I'm teaching you a process that will enable you to look to your heart and soothe your emotions, so that you can then open up and allow the inflow of good feelings into your heart. This is where Spirit lives within you, and it always feels good when Spirit inflows.*

*After reading this paragraph, feel free to put the book aside . . . get comfortable . . . tune in to your breathing . . . and the feelings in your heart . . . and gently begin to reflect upon your experiences of Spirit touching your life. Without judging yourself, gently notice if you feel open, right now, to allowing Jesus' presence to come flowing into your heart . . .*

 Pause & Experience

# 3

# From Sin . . . to Love

When looking with the dispassionate eyes of psychology at the either-or choices thrust upon traditional Christians, none seems more important than accepting and loving yourself just as you are, perfect in the eyes of God, versus chronically judging yourself as a hopeless sinner in the eyes of God. The truth is, you can't do both. The Gospels themselves in different places preach two separate paths. So the question of this chapter is: Should we choose the liberating path that emerges from the heart or the constricting path that emerges from the intellect?

Unfortunately, much of traditional Christian theology is grounded in the psychologically devastating judgment that we are all born hopeless sinners, that this is our human nature.

According to ruling theologians, God finally had compassion on the human race and sent Jesus the Christ to earth specifically to save us from our inherent sinful nature. In this scenario, God inseminated an earthly woman and thus created a child who was half god and half human. Then, knowing beforehand what he wanted to happen, he tweaked history into motion so that his only begotten son would end up being brutally sacrificed through most foul public murder.

Via the physical enactment of this ultimate celestial sacrifice, all our mortal sins were to be somehow washed away. Rather than going to hell because of our inherent sinful nature, we would be saved and would even get to go to heaven, but only if we accepted that (1) we are hopeless sinners by our very nature and (2) God actually manipulated history so as to play out the sacrifice ritual that would save us from ourselves.

I remember being told as a young child about this violent blood sacrifice of God's only begotten son. The gruesome imagery filled my mind with a most terrible childhood agony and despair. Was I such a terrible person at the core of my youthful being that such a wonderful loving person as Jesus had to be murdered so that my sins would be washed away? The guilt that overwhelmed my young heart was staggering. And then came the Communion ceremony of traditional Christianity, in which I was supposed to experience eating Jesus' body and drinking his blood – yikes!

> I've worked with many therapy clients over the years who suffered greatly, even as adults, from this early childhood programming that they're spiritually rotten to their core. I feel we should openly protest the devastating psychological consequences of inflicting such terrible trauma on children.

I know I'm speaking directly against the tradition of the church here, and if I offend any readers, all I can say is, please hear me out and then decide for yourself. Because psychologically, the reality is clear: As long as you perceive yourself as inherently damaged and hopelessly sinful and guilty at your core of being, there's not much hope of you being able to transcend your guilt and negative self-image and open to loving yourself.

In a faith based on love, does believing that you're unlovable make any sense? Jesus said clearly, "Love your neighbor as you love yourself." But if you hate yourself for being rotten to your core, that means you will hate your neighbor equally.

Contrast that scenario to Jesus' saying that we should love one another as he has loved us. There's a contradiction here, as there is throughout the Gospels, between what seems to be Jesus' message from his heart and the priestly theology stuck into the Gospels, which is based on abstract fear-based ideas rather than deeper love-based spiritual realization. I've found that only when this self-hate dimension of Christianity is discarded is the true power of Jesus' heart path released to become active in our lives.

Yes, you can believe that you escape the curse of your sinful birthright by agreeing to believe the entire theology based on this sin-redemption theology. But in so doing, you are being forced to accept the initial premise that your human nature is sinful. That act of perceiving your nature as rotten to the core will directly undermine your ability to enter into direct communion with Jesus and God. You will have sold your soul to the church and lost your freedom to explore your spiritual nature beyond the theology you've agreed to live by.

> We can't be operating in acceptance/love mode and judgment/sin mode at the same time. Psychologically, the two choices are incompatible. I'd like to explore with you what it's like to choose to live in acceptance and love, rather than judgment and sin.

I've written an entire book on this topic, called *Quiet Your Mind*, in which I show within the context of cognitive science that the judgmental function of the mind must be purposefully quieted, at least temporarily, in order for the mind to shift from head to heart and tune in to feelings of compassion. You simply can't judge yourself and love yourself at the same time.

The Gospels show us the heart path that Jesus taught. He commanded that we learn to accept and love ourselves unconditionally, as we are, and that we love others as we love ourselves – and as he loves us.

> Love itself is the one power that can wipe out the entire concept of sin, if we let go of theological concepts that close our hearts, and open up to the experience of the inflow of love in our lives.

## Love Is What Saves Us

A living relationship with the spirit of Jesus in our lives can free us, not from our "sinful" nature, but from the belief that although we're not perfect, we are perfectly lovable, just as we are. From my experience, we don't need Jesus to suffer and die for our sins in order to be free from our sense of being hopeless sinners. What we do need is Jesus' unconditional love flowing into our hearts, to give us the confidence, power, and guidance to take that leap beyond our negative theological programming into the embrace of God's love.

Built directly into salvation theology is the Christian curse of an inescapable guilt complex. I remember how agonizing were the pain and guilt I felt in my own heart as a boy because I believed that Jesus had died for my sins. I hadn't asked him to do that, but my minister convinced me that that's what happened anyway. I was such a terrible sinful creature that Jesus had to suffer his most agonizing death, so that somehow my own sinful nature would die and I would be reborn as a purified Christian. Not only did I feel guilty for being sinful, I also felt personally guilty for the death of my spiritual master.

I wonder if you went through this guilt experience yourself. It's certainly inescapable if you buy into traditional Christian theology. And of course the dynamic of the ensuing sales pitch is masterful, and goes like this: (1) We are hopeless sinners; (2) We caused God to sacrifice his only begotten Son to save us from our sinful natures; (3) Only by accepting the entire theological belief system of the church and surrendering our soul to Christ can we escape our sinful natures and somehow make Jesus' sacrifice worthwhile. If he died for our sins and we don't accept him as our lord and savior, we're doubly guilt-ridden, right?

All I can say is, where is the love? Where is the compassion? Where is God's perfect creation? And furthermore, who came up with this intellectual concept that we are born as hopeless sinners? Do you know? I spent *four years* in graduate school looking for the source of that type of belief system, and all I found to verify the belief were words in books.

> Yes, there's a certain immaculate logic to the Christian theology of sin, sacrifice, and redemption. It's a dandy philosophy in and of itself. But when we look to the core premises of the belief, do we find the spirit of Jesus there?

I didn't. And because I didn't, I felt I had to let go of the prevailing church theology in order to embrace what was supposed to lie at the heart of that theology – God's living presence. I also felt that I must speak the truth as I saw it, and stand up against a priestly cult that would turn the living gospel of Jesus' heart path into a guilt-ridden theology of human sacrifice. In this same theological thrust, the priestly cult burned at the stake anyone who dared defy their dictums. What an amazing development – that from a teaching of pure love and acceptance could evolve an institution that in the name of that teaching would brutally murder everyone who would not specifically accept what the priestly cult demanded.

> Nowadays of course, those brutal religious times are over. But – are they? In whose name did we attack Vietnam, or Iraq? George W. Bush claims to have prayed to his Christian God and been told that it would be spiritually okay to go and

kill over a hundred thousand Iraqi citizens in the name of Christ. Just how long are we going to continue this charade?

When I was in college, I very much wanted to go into politics and serve my country as best I could. I wanted to perhaps even become president so that I could use that power to help move our country in more spiritually sound directions. But once I had let go of traditional Christian beliefs and openly stated my post-Christian feelings, there was no hope of my ever being elected to major public office. Americans still insist that their leaders bow to the priestly cult's belief system. If you don't go to church, forget a political career. The church (more and more in its radical born-again garb) still rules. It is to be hoped that, in the coming years, the pendulum will finally swing in favor of leaders who lead from the heart rather than from the pocketbook.

Of course, many politicians try to lead from their hearts, and many born-again ministers try to preach love instead of hate. What I'm pointing out is that at the heart of our Christian religion lie basic assumptions and beliefs about God and human nature that pollute our decisions and drag our decisions down into fear-based reactions that go directly against Jesus' deeper teachings.

## Compassion versus Morality

While we're on this general topic, let's talk specifically about the inherent perversion of trying to live "moral" lives. In America especially, this is a giant term that underlies our culture. The religious right even tried to identify itself as "the moral majority," as if the remaining minority were, by definition, immoral. But what does it really mean to be moral? And how does trying to live a moral life either sustain or undermine a deep spiritual life?

Most people assume that it's our moral character that keeps us from doing bad things. This assumption is based on the Christian notion that our underlying nature is evil and must be constantly controlled by our moral restric-

tions. But is this negative self-judgment a valid psychological assumption about human nature?

When seen from a dispassionate spiritual perspective, the moral path appears actually to be the opposite of the spiritual path. When you walk the path of morality, you walk the path of judgment – trying to do what is judged as right and avoid doing what is judged as wrong. The moral path is, on careful observation, the very path where the concept of sin arises.

Most cultures have developed a code of right and wrong behavior, and morality is the result. This is the path of "shoulds" and "shouldn'ts." A good person does what the society has deemed to be right and avoids doing (or even thinking about doing) what society considers wrong or evil. This is the fear-based approach to living, where our decisions are made based on the fear of what would happen if we violated the accepted moral codes.

The spiritual path, as I see it, is just the opposite: This is a path where your actions are not determined by what you should or shouldn't do according to the morality of the ruling priests and judges or your own fear-based judgments.

In a spiritually rather than morally grounded life, your decisions and actions emerge from an opposite direction. You allow Spirit and your deeper connectedness with God's wisdom and love to determine what you do each moment. On the spiritual path, love in your heart, not the judgment of your intellect, guides you.

In our culture, our morals are mostly dictated by traditional Christian beliefs, rules, and regulations. These rules and regulations originated in the Old Testament. The Ten Commandments are key to this moral base. The Jewish tradition was steeped in morality, as are most traditions. The Jewish priestly cult dictated what was right and what was wrong, and anything they decided was wrong was called a sin. It was a sin to walk beyond a certain distance on the Sabbath, for instance, a sin to eat the wrong foods, and a sin even to think the wrong thoughts.

Jesus found himself regularly caught up in arguments with priests about sin, morality, right and wrong. He was hollered at for hanging out with sinners rather than with the righteous, and he often did things that the priests considered wrong. Over and over, he tried to explain that he was guided not by moral rules but by his spontaneous heart response to each new situation.

We are *still* struggling to break out of the morality of the Old Testament and truly embrace the radical new spirituality of Jesus' words and example. I remember being an idealistic young minister in San Francisco during the Vietnam War. The church that employed me was a bastion of conservative wealthy members who supported the war wholeheartedly and, in many cases, made loads of money from our being at war. And the judgment was clear: All Communists are evil, Communism is an evil movement, and Christianity must rise up and obliterate it, even though the battlefield was halfway around the world from our country.

> Somehow within their Christian belief system, most members of the church felt it was perfectly fine to go off and kill innocent women and children in the name of Christ and all things good, moral, and Christian.

I gave just one sermon on this topic. I stood up, put my sermon notes aside, and spoke from the heart about my understanding of Jesus' teachings and how sending one's sons to Vietnam to murder people didn't quite make sense morally or otherwise. After all, wasn't one of the primary sins taking another human's life?

But no, it seems that I didn't quite understand Christian theology correctly. After my sermon, I received a number of lectures about how sometimes it's necessary to bend the laws and sometimes it's moral to kill people – we should even feel good about it! During the Bush-Kerry presidential campaign in 2004, the same issue came up. American boys had gone over to a foreign country that hadn't even attacked us and, in just one year, had killed over a hundred thousand people, and somehow we were supposed to feel that this murdering rampage was morally okay?

I mention all this because, ultimately, the logic of theology and morality always breaks down. The most horrendous deeds have been blessed as entirely moral by the priestly cult in the name of Christ. So what are we to do?

Here's a clue. Morality emerges from the judgmental function of the human mind – what is right to do, and what is wrong. It's all about the process of intellectual debate and reason deciding what is a sin, and what isn't. And ultimately, from a spiritual perspective, living one's life based on such intellectual judgment just doesn't work. The sad truth is that we can talk ourselves into doing all sorts of things and calling them moral, and we can feel guilty for doing certain things that our society condemns, even though, in our hearts, our actions feel good and right.

Therefore I don't find religious morality a functional concept for living a spiritual life, and have long ago discarded the whole idea. I don't try to live a moral life. I don't continually judge what I do by the standards of the church. Instead, I've found that there's a vastly better way to negotiate life.

Jesus said very clearly, "Judge not!" And as we'll see later, this is one of his primary dictums that must be taken seriously. If we're to advance beyond external regulations and morals into a life where our present-moment actions feel right in our hearts and souls, we must let go of living out of judgment, and advance into living our lives immersed in the wisdom and motivation of Spirit.

We have the power to stop judging and, instead, to accept others just as they are, neither good nor bad, neither sinful or righteous, but, rather, creatures with whom we are in relationship through love. And the same surely goes for ourselves. We have the choice, the power, and the mental capacity to love ourselves just as we are. Until we let go of judging ourselves, we are unable to open up to the inflow of love and spiritual guidance in our hearts.

Conversely, when we do finally love ourselves just as we are, without judgment, we gain access to that deep voice that speaks from our hearts and guides us in all that we think and do. When love rather than morality becomes our guiding light, our actions become transformed. When we learn to regularly allow Spirit to live in our hearts and guide our actions, then and only then do we become truly moral beings in the higher sense of knowing what is right action and doing it.

Perhaps this sounds like a great challenge – to stop judging and accept ourselves just as we are – but you'll find in this book all the spiritual and psychological tools you'll need in order to make this leap into a loving relationship with yourself. It's actually not hard at all. You simply must regularly choose to accept and forgive yourself, and then move on.

## The Power to Forgive

Yes, we transcend guilt and self-judgment through the power of acceptance and forgiveness. Jesus told us to love one another as he loves us, which means unconditionally, without any judgment at all. This is the basis of the act of forgiveness: that we totally accept what we have done.

From a psychological point of view, there are giant gaps in logic in the Gospels when it comes to forgiveness. When I read the Gospels, I sometimes experience the realization that certain words I'm reading do not make spiritual sense at all. I know it's heresy to say so, but there are entire chapters of the Gospels whose authenticity I strongly question.

> What are we to do when we read the Gospels and, at certain places, feel a disconnection with Jesus' loving presence in the words? Must we reject what our hearts tell us, or let go of what the Bible tells us? Again, we're right on the edge of the kind of heresy that used to get people burned at the stake – but there's no looking away from this.

Jesus most clearly told his followers, "Know the truth, and the truth will set you free." To know the truth is to look to your heart, tune in to your spiritual wisdom, and receive insight from your spiritual core of being. In this spirit, I have definitely felt moved to let go of certain sayings in the Bible that my heart and soul cannot resonate with, that do not match the experience I've had of Jesus' presence directly in my life.

I don't feel that Jesus judged everyone around him as hopeless sinners. The theology of the church doesn't match the words of Jesus' mouth. He didn't say *judge* one another, he said *love* one another. And he didn't say hate yourself for being a terrible person, he said open up and let love fill your heart. When you do that, forgiveness naturally happens.

I cannot accept forgiveness from others unless I have first forgiven myself. And once I forgive myself, I don't really need the forgiveness of others. This is a psychological fact that all therapists can verify from working with clients. When people judge themselves for doing something wrong in the past and heap guilt on themselves, seeing themselves as hopeless sinners, the only hope for them is to come to the point where they let go of the self-judgment and forgive themselves for what they've done.

A deeper healing process happens when we break through the grip of self-judgment and, in the act of accepting what we have done in the past, allow love to come flowing again into our hearts. Before we can open up to Spirit, there is this essential step we must make, and not even Jesus can make that step for us. We must forgive ourselves.

No one, not even Jesus, can force us to open our hearts to love. Love will heal the guilt, but we must first take the step of forgiving ourselves before the love can come into our hearts. Do you see this? Have you experienced it? And do you see the inherent manipulation of the theology that says you *can't* forgive yourself, you must ask Jesus to forgive you? It violates the basic psychological principles of how our minds work, principles that, surely, God set up in the first place.

The entire sin/forgiveness thrust of the Gospels, in which the act and responsibility of forgiveness are taken away from us and placed elsewhere, strikes me as yet another priestly power play that was written into the Gospels, quite some time after Jesus was gone from this Earth.

Hold in mind that at least 50 to 60 years passed before Jesus' sayings and actions were written down, at least in the four gospel versions that were included in the formal Bible. And these gospels weren't written in the spirit of simply documenting Jesus' life; the intent of writing them was to solidify a particular theological understanding of what Jesus' life meant at philosophical and esoteric levels.

The new priests of the Christian religion were struggling to establish a new theology, a new morality, a new belief system to implant in their followers. So, naturally, they wanted a gospel that would promote their theology.

And so in my understanding, the writers of these gospels often put into Jesus' mouth what they wanted him to have said, just as much as or more than what they thought he said, based on third- or fourth-generation word-of-mouth accounts.

I say all this because, if you are going to base your life on certain words, concepts, and theological attitudes in the Bible, you're going to be hopelessly stuck when it comes to sin and forgiveness. As long as you believe that you can't forgive yourself, that you have to ask Jesus the Christ to forgive you, then good luck. Because there's a psychological flaw in the theology that you'll never get beyond.

If you expect someone else to do the forgiving rather than yourself, you might remain a hopeless sinner all your life. As a traditional Christian, you can remain stuck in guilt over Jesus the Christ dying for your sins. And you'll probably continue to judge yourself as a sinner who continually violates the moral laws and thus forces Jesus to forgive you again and again.

For me, this is not the spiritual path, this is the morality highway. Your choice is to exit the highway – by letting go of the notion that you are a hopeless sinner. Jesus said to the woman, "Go and sin no more." I humbly say the same thing to you: Sin no more. And how do you do that? By letting go altogether of the notion of being a sinner.

Jesus provided two utterly powerful and transforming dictums that ring with authenticity and exactly define how to sin no more. He said, "Stop judging," first of all, and, indeed, if you stop judging yourself as a sinner, you have transcended sin. He also said, "Be ye therefore perfect, even as your Father in heaven is perfect."

He's actually ordering you to stop judging yourself as an imperfect sinner, and advance spiritually to where you realize you are indeed perfect, beyond judgment – just as you are. You are God's creation. How can a perfect infinite spiritual Creator create something that is imperfect?

All that separates you from your perfection is your own judgmental mind. You are the one who is judging you. And therefore you are the one who must stop it.

> Stop judging yourself as a sinner, and instead love yourself just as you are, as God's perfect creation, right here, right now. Set yourself free. Forgive yourself once and for all. And let the love flow in.

Here's the primary payoff in all this: When you love yourself unconditionally and accept yourself just as you are, you make it possible for Spirit to live in your heart. And when Spirit lives in your heart and guides your actions, you can do no wrong. Sure, you'll do things that are foolish, you'll goof up now and then. This is only human. We learn from our mistakes – as long as we don't reject them.

With Spirit in your heart, you'll love yourself when you goof up. You'll have compassion for yourself when you give in to temptation. You'll love yourself as Jesus loves you – beyond the touch of sin altogether. This, for me, is our aim. This is our spiritual destiny.

I'm aware that my tone of voice throughout this first part of the book is quite emphatic and passionate. I had originally set out to write this first section dispassionately, but I found that my emotions were engaged as I discussed these seven basic choices with you. The logic of the discussion is so strong inside me that I can't speak of these realizations that have so touched my soul without passion coming into my writing voice. I do hope that my passion doesn't feel like pressure. But I want to make sure you realize that church dogma can indeed be questioned by rational, good-hearted people and that there is a choice between religious tradition and our emerging psychologically grounded future.

## ✿ Reflection Time

*We've explored several very hot topics in this chapter. Again, I wonder what's going on in your mind. In all fairness, it's time for me to be entirely quiet and give you plenty of space to reflect on your own evolving feelings on these themes. So let's pause and end this chapter with another reflection break – put down the book, relax, get comfortable, and observe what's going on, in your mind and especially in your heart.*

*Feel free to put the book aside after reading this paragraph . . . stretch and give yourself permission to feel good in your body . . . tune in to the air flowing in and out of your nose . . . the movements in your chest and belly as you breathe. Expand your awareness to include the feelings in your heart, right in the middle of your breathing . . . and as you hold your attention on your breathing and your heart, say to yourself a few times, "I love myself, just as I am." Explore what it feels like to accept and forgive yourself, and feel good and whole in the eyes of God . . . be open to whatever thoughts and feelings come to you . . . breathe into them . . . be open to a new experience!*

 **Pause & Reflect**

# 4

# From Priests . . . to Magdalena

We now come to a quite remarkable and ultimately unavoidable choice. Christianity soon turned into a patriarchal religious organization led by men who excluded women from positions of influence and power. The Gospels seem to have been edited accordingly, so as to minimize the role and influence of women. Whatever more feminine dimensions of Jesus' teaching there might have been were removed, so as to make possible and even seemingly inevitable the male-dominated religion.

Yes, as the centuries went by and the populace hungered for their old-time female gods of the pantheon, the Catholic Church went ahead and allowed Jesus' mother to become the female representative of the story.

But the Holy Trinity – the Father, the Son, and the Holy Ghost – remained male or neutral. The pope remained unquestionably male, as did the priests who represented Jesus Christ in all church ceremonies. A healthy balanced feminine dimension to Christian theology never came into being.

A close look at the Inquisition shows that almost all of the seven million people who were murdered by the church authorities were women.

The Inquisition was a massive horrendous religious war against all things feminine. In this light, Christians, Jews, and Moslems all have in common a tradition and a theology that not only deny the feminine principle as equal to the masculine, but actively subjugate and, when required, openly persecute their women.

I feel we need to look at this reality and do something about it in our own hearts and lives. In this chapter, we'll initiate an exploration in this direction, then in later chapters learn concrete meditative ways to balance male and female in our own inner realms, and encourage this balance in the world around us.

But first, to show you a primary if unusual source of my feelings in regard to Christianity and the feminine, I'd like to share with you a dream I had at seminary that powerfully influenced my life. I'm not saying that this dream necessarily reflected historical reality, but it emerged from such a deep place within me that I was jolted out of my acceptance of Christianity's traditional masculine dominance. You'll perhaps note that there is considerable similarity between my dream and the Black Madonna tradition recently dramatized in novels such as *The Da Vinci Code*. But at that point in my life, having just arrived at seminary, I'd never heard of any hidden tradition about Jesus and Maria Magdalena being sexual partners nor about the possibility of Jesus having genetic heirs. So the dream was a shock to me.

## Magdalena in Prison

In the dream I was walking through a vast forest of cedar trees, enjoying the mountain scent in the air, listening to the birds, watching a doe and her fawn walk quietly away from my approach. I was on a trail that led me deeper and higher for quite some time, until suddenly, I came to a small clearing and saw a hut in front of me. I ducked off to one side so as not to be seen and the following is what I observed, somehow knowing who was who through the knowledge that often accompanies dream sequences.

As I watched, the door to the hut opened and a woman came walking out, looking up to the sky where storm clouds were just beginning to approach the mountains from the west. The woman was about six or seven months pregnant. I knew immediately that she was Maria Magdalena, Jesus' special woman friend. The shock of seeing her pregnant was amplified by my somehow being certain that she was pregnant by Jesus himself, even though he was now four or five months dead and gone.

At first, I felt an amazing elation at realizing that Magdalena was pregnant with Jesus' child. But then I saw the anxious haggard look on her face and my spirits dropped instantly. She came walking fearfully out of the hut, holding a fairly heavy cloth satchel in hand. Not seeing anyone around the hut, she suddenly took off running for all she was worth – right past where I was hiding.

I wanted to step out and offer her my support; it was clear that she was fearful, in danger, and trying to make an escape. But as often happens in dreams, my feet were leaden; I couldn't shout or run after her. Instead, I sat down in the forest for a few minutes, drifting away from the drama I'd just witnessed, watching a bug working diligently to move a smaller dead bug through the dirt at my feet.

Suddenly, my nerves were jolted by the sound of angry voices coming back up the trail. I glanced and saw two men rough-handling Maria Magdalena, dragging her back to the hut. I

45

wanted to jump up and come to her rescue, but again my body wouldn't go into action.

Obviously against her wishes, though she remained silent, the two men pushed her into the hut and slammed the door on her. I knew somehow who they were – Jesus' apostles Peter and James. I could overhear their private conversation as they came walking closer toward my hiding place. James was upset by the thought that Maria Magdalena would have been killed by the Romans if she'd managed to return to the lowlands. She was acting so foolishly.

Peter agreed, but I could see that his intent was more ominous than simply holding Magdalena hostage for her own good. He was adamant that her pregnancy was a threat to everything Jesus had attempted to bring into being with his teachings. There must be no genetic heir to Jesus' throne. Probably the woman wasn't even pregnant with Jesus' child, he mumbled – she had always been a troublemaker, coming between Jesus and his true disciples.

And now there was a large following of people down below who were searching for Magdalena, believing she was their new spiritual leader. No, Peter insisted – she must be removed somehow, forever. If she gave birth to Jesus' child, all would be lost.

James was of a different inner mind, even though he promised Peter he would make sure she didn't escape. Peter had something important he had to do down in Galilee for a few weeks. James assured him that Magdalena would be safe and secure here in the hut, with James standing guard. Peter was uncertain, but he had other bothersome things on his mind and finally agreed, stomping off and away from the hut, headed down to the lowlands. James watched him disappear. I could see the deeply concerned expression on his face as he then turned and hurried into the hut.

Time went by. My attention again drifted to simple sensory pleasures all around me. But then a cloud came between me and the sun and a chill breeze picked up, rushing through the tops of the cedar trees high above me. I stood up, realizing that a storm was coming and I'd better head down the mountain. But just as I was turning to leave, the door to the hut opened again.

James came outside, looked around suspiciously, and then called to the woman. Magdalena came hesitantly out into the chill of the afternoon, with her satchel in hand. They looked toward the trail where Peter had departed some time before. Then quite urgently, they looked into each other's eyes, then walked together around the hut in the other direction, and started up a rough trail that led over to the other side of the mountain.

I wanted to shout out to them that the storm was coming, that they should wait until it passed, but again I had no power to interfere with history – I could only remain mute and watch the two of them disappear into the thick forest. Soon they were gone. The wind picked up stronger. I stood up and started hurrying down the path I'd come up, the same path that Peter had taken, down from the mountain toward the lowlands.

## Black Madonna Rising

I woke up from the dream with a start. Standing beside my bed when I opened my eyes was a beautiful dark-haired pregnant woman, her big belly looking just like Maria Magdalena's had looked. At first I was confused, but then I realized that what I'd experienced had only been a dream. The pregnant woman now before me was my own wife, six months pregnant with my own first child. I had a lecture to attend in less than half an hour and she was waking me up so I wouldn't be late. I mumbled something about not feeling well and rolled over, covering myself with my blankets, drifting back into that dream that had been so real I could hardly discern the difference between that reality and this waking one.

The dream wouldn't leave me alone. Having been brought up Protestant, without even a Mother Mary to worship like the

Catholics have, I had never thought much about what happened to Maria Magdalena after Jesus was killed. Nor had I ventured much imagination regarding whether or not Jesus and Maria Magdalena had been platonic friends or indeed, as in the dream, intimate sexual partners.

> But now the idea wouldn't leave my head – I was consumed with the notion that this young devoted woman who had obviously been platonically close to Jesus, as noted in the Gospels, might have been even more. Might have been vastly more.

I found myself in the depths of the seminary library, discovering old texts that talked considerably about Maria Magdalena – most in hostile terms. I discovered that there was a strong although much-suppressed tradition that believed that Maria Magdalena, pregnant with Jesus' child, had escaped to Gaul, in the southern part of France, and there given birth to Jesus' son. A powerful spiritual tradition and religious organization had come into being there, based on the genetic heirs to Jesus' throne.

At the heart of this tradition was what the books called "The Black Madonna," referring to Maria Magdalena. The Catholic Church had seen her as an evil force fighting against their dominance in the world.

This tradition of the historical Black Madonna has recently been popularized by books, media programs, and church discussions. It does seem probable that the story might be true, even though historians lack enough evidence to be sure. But what struck me to the core in my dream and in my explorations of this hidden tradition was the uplifting vision of Jesus not as a solitary man surrounded by his 12 male disciples, but merged with a powerful sexual and spiritual partner of distinctly feminine wiles and integrity who balanced all dimensions of his life and teaching.

> At seminary, as I let this possibility take root inside me, I realized that for Jesus to be the primary spiritual presence

in my life, I needed an equal feminine spiritual presence.
And I suddenly realized what I'd been missing spiritually all
my life: the feminine half of the Christian equation.

I myself was soon to become a father, I was in love and happily
mated, and I knew firsthand how coming together with a woman
had transformed me. The idea of Jesus having been likewise
transformed through a sexual and spiritual union with Maria
Magdalena not only made perfect sense, it also became a spiritual
necessity.

## The Feminine Touch

Then one evening while I was meditating, it happened. I was sitting there progressing through the same basic meditation that I'm
going to teach you (although it has advanced since those early
days) and I felt Jesus' presence coming into my heart. Suddenly, I
felt something more coming into my awareness. I won't try to
describe what I felt because it's impossible to put adequately into
words – also, I want you to have your own experience, if you
haven't already. Suffice it to say I felt a feminine presence flowing
into my heart along with Jesus' masculine presence. And for the
first time in a deep spiritual way, I felt . . . whole.

> Ever since, whenever I open to Jesus' presence, I also open
> to Magdalena's. The combination of these two seems to be
> what constitutes the Holy Spirit for me at experiential lev-
> els. I simply cannot spiritually imagine Jesus without Maria
> with him. Together they are one.

In contrast, without Magdalena in the theological equation, the
traditional church has been dangerously lopsided in the masculine direction. It's rather amazing in these contemporary times to
realize that the Catholic tradition still refuses even to consider a
female pope or ecclesiastic leader. And I found the Presbyterian
church almost equally dominated not only by men, but also by

masculine attitudes. The heart path is almost nonexistent in the Protestant tradition, and all things considered feminine, such as tenderness, receptivity, intuitive guidance, and spiritual nurturing, have a difficult time growing in the masculine atmosphere.

Great spiritually attuned psychologists such as Carl Jung have written quite eloquently (and correctly) about the dangers of masculine-dominated organizations. In business, certainly (which is where I'm working mostly these days), the old-time notion that success comes from being coldhearted and aggressive, rather than warmhearted and cooperative, is being rapidly pushed aside in favor of a more heartful approach to business. Capitalism is the consummate expression of too much masculine and not enough feminine in the equation – and if we don't do something to gain a healthy male-female balance in the global economy, it's obvious the ecological world is doomed. (Check out www.selbysolution.com if this specific theme attracts you.)

But equally important is the danger of male-female imbalance to our mental and spiritual health. Traditional Christian upbringing tends to develop seriously imbalanced personalities in both men and women. Holding on to a priestly belief in which the Trinity is all male and no female can be disastrous to the soul. And shifting into a balanced male-female meditative experience can save one's soul.

> So again, you have the choice: in this case, to continue to believe and support theologies that reinforce masculine dominance of your psyche, or to let go of such beliefs and embrace a new vision of wholeness in the male-female equation.

Obviously there have been many instances in Christian history where the feminine has been supported and at least temporary balance achieved. My intent here isn't to judge; my intent is to point your attention toward an important aspect of church doctrine and let you decide for yourself what is most healthy for your future spiritual growth.

The feminine touch is clearly a powerful touch. I'm suggesting the development of a meditation practice in which you regularly bring that feminine touch into your spiritual life. The most direct way to do this is through including Maria Magdalena alongside Jesus in your meditation. There's no need to develop any grand new theology around this male-female union. Rather than thinking about it, just do it!

## Thinking in a New Way

Often in this book, you'll find me making statements like the preceding one, in which I seem to be putting down the human thought process in favor of a quiet mind and an active experiential focus. Please don't get me wrong – I love and respect our higher mental functions. But I make a distinction between thinking that is mostly robotic, based on childhood programming and unquestioned beliefs, and thinking that is inspired, emerging from a deeper place than our usual scattered thoughts.

In this light, I very much respect the early Greek tradition in which thought was placed as the highest vehicle for attaining spiritual freedom. But the deep philosophy of that tradition was itself based on the higher reflective and intuitive functions of the thinking mind. Thought in Greek philosophy was used *to transcend thought* by holding one's attention on a particular theme and looking more and more deeply into that theme, employing intuitive insight and spiritual realization as part of the thinking discipline.

Indeed, in the meditation I will be teaching you, the first challenge is to quiet your usual chatterbox flow of thoughts, and then, in this quiet state of mind, to focus on and listen to the deeper voice that speaks to you from your core of wisdom – and to take those new thoughts very seriously indeed.

The masculine mode of thinking is active, dominant, thrusting outward, talkative, and fixated on pushing one's own attitudes and beliefs. This is the traditional Christian mode in which one's mind is dominated by ideas, theological arguments, and strident beliefs. Conversely, the feminine mode of thinking is first to listen, to be quiet and reflect, and then to surrender to the deeper voice that emerges only when regular thoughts stop.

In the New Testament, very few feminine voices are heard. Does Maria Magdalena have anything at all to say, according to the men who wrote the Gospels? And what do we really know of Jesus' mother? Such questions have no answers when we look to the church and its masculine dominance. But you can readily open up and discover the feminine qualities of your spiritual life by allowing Maria Magdalena (and any other feminine spiritual presence that might come to you) to touch your heart regularly.

# ❧ Reflection Time

*What do you think about all this? Yes, I'm playing quite a masculine role in this book, by passionately expressing my feelings about these seven choices we all face in our spiritual lives. But also, regularly, I want to stop and give you total breathing space to let the dust settle . . . put this book aside . . . and give yourself at least five minutes to tune in to your own feelings, your own ideas, your own spiritual needs and insights.*

*So here's another reflection pause . . . after reading these words, feel free to put the book aside . . . turn your attention inward to your breathing . . . your heart . . . your whole-body presence in this new moment . . . and ask yourself, what would happen to your relationship with Jesus (and with yourself) if you opened up and allowed the feminine half to be there too . . . explore how you would feel if you allowed Maria Magdalena, in her purely spiritual presence, to be included in your meditative experience . . . Allow your mind to become quiet . . . breathe . . . live within your heart . . . and allow your heart to speak its truth to you . . . be open to whatever feelings and insights come to you!*

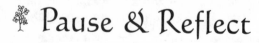 Pause & Reflect

# 5

# From Written Word . . . to Holy Spirit

Traditional Christianity rests on a strict and sometimes even fanatical devotion to the physical documentation of Jesus' life and teachings as found in the printed words of the Bible. This historical, written Word of God is the basis of all theology and dogma of the church. It's no surprise, with this constant fixation on written words and ideas, that true believers tend to get caught up *thinking about* God, rather than *experiencing* God directly in their hearts, minds, and souls.

In this chapter, I'd like to explore the deeper significance of your ongoing choice between focusing on the written Bible with its entirely past-oriented narrative, and focusing on the intimate experience of welcoming Holy Spirit into your heart and life here in this constantly emerging and eternal present moment. As we'll see, right here right now, you can open up to Spirit and know the truth directly, rather than just read about it from ancient second- and thirdhand accounts.

> Your conscious and ongoing choice to shift from being fix-ated on words and concepts in the Bible to experiencing direct communion with Spirit in your heart and mind will provide a great leap into spiritual awakening. This entire book is about this leap of faith.

## Holy Spirit

Sometimes it seems that every one of the primary spiritual terms in the Christian heritage has been so overused and abused that it's impossible to carry on a deep conversation without first clearly redefining each term being discussed. I feel this way every time I use the term "Holy Spirit," especially because the term has evolved in meaning and significance in my life so that what I mean now is noticeably advanced from how I used the term ear-lier in my life.

So to begin this crucial chapter I'd like to talk further about how I understand the terms "spirit," "Spirit," "Holy Spirit," and "Spirit of God." First, let's explore how the four Gospels use these terms. In Matthew, we hear that Maria was "found to be with child of the Holy Spirit." Likewise, Elizabeth "was filled with the Holy Spirit" and "the Holy Spirit was upon Simeon" so that he knew events of the future.

> Jesus was "filled with the Holy Spirit" and baptized his fol-lowers with the Holy Spirit. "The Holy Spirit descended upon him (Jesus) in bodily form, as a dove." And later, "Jesus, full of the Holy Spirit, returned from the Jordan, and was led by the Spirit for 40 days in the wilderness."

Jesus is said to have "rejoiced in the Holy Spirit." He also assured us that the Heavenly Father "will give the Holy Spirit to those who ask him" and "The Holy Spirit will teach you . . . what you should say . . . the Counselor, the Holy Spirit, whom the Father will send in my name, will teach you all things." In the Gospels, we find that we can be "inspired by the Holy Spirit" and that we must not "blaspheme against the Holy Spirit."

In the book of Acts, which gives an account of what happened to the disciples after Jesus was gone, there are 40 references to the Holy Spirit, in which people are "filled with the Holy Spirit" or "resist the Holy Spirit" or "receive the Holy Spirit" or are "comforted by the Holy Spirit." Disciples are "sent out by the Holy Spirit" and followers are "baptized by the Holy Spirit." Some are "forbidden by the Holy Spirit" to go and speak the gospel in Asia. Others directly hear the Holy Spirit speaking to them, or speak themselves with the words of the Holy Spirit.

> When we look in the New Testament for the term "Spirit" without the word "Holy" but with the big "S," we find that "the Spirit of the Lord" was active in the lives of the disciples. "The Spirit of Jesus" influenced people's thoughts and behavior. "The Spirit of God" touches the hearts of men.

In Matthew, we have the important quote, "When they deliver you up, do not be anxious how you are to speak or what you are to say; for what you are to say will be given to you in that hour; for it is not you who speak, but the Spirit of your Father speaking through you." Elsewhere Jesus was "inspired by the Spirit," and people can be "full of the Spirit and wisdom."

Now for the use of the term "spirit" with a small "s": There are numerous mentions of spirits, both of unclean and evil spirits, but also of the everyday spirits of human beings. We are told that "the spirit is willing, but the flesh is weak." Jesus says that "blessed are the poor in spirit, for theirs is the kingdom of heaven." Luke says, "My spirit rejoices in God." Luke also says, referring to Jesus, "The child grew and became strong in spirit." John says, "God is spirit, and those who worship him must worship in spirit and truth."

So there you have most of the important gospel references to the primary terms that refer to God's invisible yet active presence in our historical physical world. I find these references acutely parallel to my experience of how Spirit inflows into my life. There does exist a dimension of consciousness where we can open up inside and tap into direct communion with and even quite specific inspiration and guidance by a spiritual presence that ultimately is . . . God. As a psychologist, I've been exploring how this experience can be purposefully encouraged, given the particular cognitive dynamics of our minds.

Let me share with you what I've found, because this level of insight can make all the difference in providing you with the expanded conceptual model needed to confidently take the great leap of faith and open up to this dimension of consciousness. I'm going to move fairly fast in this explanation, because the nature of this book is not that of a formal psychological treatise. If you want an in-depth explanation, please go online to my www.johnselby.com site where you'll gain access to the expanded psychological discussions.

## The Subtle Touch

All too often when people talk about things spiritual, especially about the actual act of Spirit inflowing into a person's personal consciousness, the discussion becomes overly esoteric and stumbles into old clichés. Certain media-fixated born-again preachers have so overdramatized, and often made a mockery of, the inner and ultimately personal experience of Spirit inflow that many people of a more rational bent consider the whole phenomenon of Spirit inflow a sham.

We need to move beyond the abuses of this term, so we can discover the great power of the experience. I've been working for the last 35 years (ever since the actual experience of Spirit inflow happened clearly in my heart and mind) to gain a psychological understanding of what's actually happening in the mind when mind and Spirit meet. Often this is a subtle experience in meditation, not at all an explosive media-friendly drama.

> I personally find that the deeper I get into the merger of mind and spirit as an integrated experience, the less dramatic the experience becomes. This, after all, is our natural state: to live our lives with our spiritual quality unified with all the rest of our mental function.

So please put away all the stereotypes of people rolling around on the floor screaming in delightful mystical agony as they seem to get almost sexually tormented by the inflow of Spirit into their bodies. I don't stick my nose in other people's business enough to question what sort of experience they are having, genuine or otherwise. But I assure you that, usually, from my observation, the experience of being touched by the Holy Spirit is remarkably quiet and subtle.

In fact often the challenge is being sensitive enough to realize what's happening. Much of the meditation process I'm going to teach you is designed to help you quiet your usual busy mental and emotional activity, so that you can tune in to what's happening at deeper spiritual levels.

## Where Mind and Spirit Meet

To gain a clearer understanding of how mind and spirit unite, we first need to clarify the basic psychological playing field within which all this happens. Each of us naturally possesses a quality of mind that we call awareness, or consciousness. We are organisms like all other organisms, able to perceive the environment around us through our sensory organs, and also our inner environment.

Right now you're reading these words through your visual awareness. You're aware of your own three-dimensional body in the here and now of the present moment. You have your senses of hearing, of taste, of touch, and of smell to make you aware of certain dimensions of the physical world. You also have nerves in your muscles and tissue that enable you to have a physical sense of self-awareness, and to experience the flow of emotions in your body.

Thus you are a conscious entity in the universe – within the limits of your senses. Since time immemorial, however, people have reported experiences that lie beyond the standard physical senses. We speak of people who have a sixth sense, for instance, and talk about feelings that transcend the emotional. There are a host of spiritual experiences that seem entirely real to the people who have them, yet which cannot be described in the context of perceptual psychology. The experience of being touched by or filled with or spoken to by or guided by the Holy Spirit is one of these ineffable yet very real experiences that science can't get a handle on; yet from the inside, we know the experience to be real.

What is actually happening in the mind to enable, generate, or receive such a "spiritual" experience? To answer this, we need to understand that the brain possesses a special but quite natural function very different from its usual activity of processing sensory information and then thinking about that sensory information at a conceptual level. We also have the vast right-brain region of our brain that is usually referred to as intuitive or creative, and it seems that this region of the brain is the receptor of input that is of a more subtle nature than our usual perceptual input.

> The intuitive-creative function of the brain is designed to perceive the whole rather than fixating on points in space. It's also designed to function only in the present moment, rather than drifting off into past or future. This region of the brain is tuned in intensely and intimately to the here and now, where Spirit is experienced.

The intuitive function of the mind is centered in the right brain, but we're discovering in brain research that our intuitive-creative function is actually a whole-brain happening. Brain scans reveal that during an intuitive flash, the whole brain seems to light up; this is how we see the whole at once, know from our depths the truth of something, and experience moments in which we transcend our usual sense of who we are. Even without venturing into "spiritual" realms at all, we possess an immense mental capacity to flash with present-moment realization and insight.

What's held my interest strongly recently is new research showing that the intuitive function of the mind isn't just a function of the four brains nestled together in the skull. The heart has been found to contain nerve tissue almost identical to the brain's, and there's constant communication between the heart and the brain, so much so that researchers are more and more calling the heart the fifth brain. There are massive neural pathways for communication between heart and brain, with information passing both ways nonstop.

> Scientists are beginning to be able to understand neurologically why people report that they can "speak from their heart" and "know in their heart" what is true in a situation or what they should do in life. The heart is the center of our emotional experience, surely, and more and more seems to be the center of our deeper intuitive experience as well.

In fact, scientists are now expanding their definition of the brain to include not just the heart, but also the stomach and intestines, which interact so intimately with the brain, and also the largest organ of the body, the skin, which is a vast neurological presence with neural matter very similar to that found in the brain.

## When Thoughts about God Become Quiet

What seems clear at this point, both from studies of meditation and neurological investigations, is that we have the potential to function either in our normal mode of consciousness (in which we're usually lost in thought, memories, imagining, or problem-solving) or in a more expanded state of consciousness. And it is when we're in this expanded, intuitive, whole-body state of awareness in the present moment that experiences of a more ephemeral yet no less impactful quality come to us.

> You have this capacity naturally. We're exploring here the most effective ways for consciously shifting into intuitive-spiritual mode, so that you regularly move yourself into position to receive input from your higher mind and from the even deeper realms of spiritual wisdom and empowerment.

In a nutshell, here's what we've found: As long as we're in "broadcast" mode, in which we're thinking up a storm, lost in the past of memories, or lost in the future of imaginings, we're not in "receive" mode at all. Spirit can't touch us. As long as our ego is dominating the scene, we're locked into our ego games, which limit our consciousness to our programmed set of expectations, beliefs, attitudes, compulsions, and all the rest of the ego-based mental functions. As long as our thinking mind is noisily broadcasting its own presence, the mind is not able to receive input from beyond the ego bubble.

> Only when we quiet our thoughts, only when we temporarily silence our own agitations, worries, and power plays, does our mind attain that state of calm, peace, trust, and receptivity required for Spirit to inflow.

Therefore it's obvious that thinking about God, or getting caught in one theological argument or another, goes directly against the opportunity to open up to our spiritual levels of consciousness. Meditation outside any religious dogma is the process through which we quiet our thinking minds, by moving our focus away from the past and the future toward the present moment experience that's happening right here, right now.

There is always the clear and vital choice before us from the point of view of consciousness management, of focusing on words and thoughts about God (reading the Bible, for instance) or focusing on present-moment experience in which Spirit can flow into our minds and hearts and touch us directly.

I'm not saying that we must forever stop thinking – just the opposite. I'm saying that we need to learn how to quiet our everyday mental chatter, shift from cognitive to intuitive mode in our minds, and then through the touch of Spirit in our minds allow a flow of inspired thoughts, which will be of an entirely different quality from our usual fear-and-power level of thought-flows.

## Written Word as Launch Pad

There are two completely different ways of approaching the Bible, which is often referred to as the written Word of God. We can read the words in the Bible in order to develop an even more complex intellectual system that defines in concepts and symbols our theological beliefs about God. Or we can read the words in the Bible in order to discover key statements that point our mind's attention beyond words and concepts, toward God as an experience in the present moment. Many people find themselves doing both. They read the Bible (or some other book), seeking clarity and meaning, but at some point, they find that their minds shift naturally from cognitive to intuitive and, for a moment or more, thoughts become silent and an experience comes to them.

> Right at this point, where thoughts stop while one is reading and a flash of insight and realization comes, the Bible ceases to be a theological text and becomes a meditative launch pad.

In my observation, it is this sudden flash of heart-centered feeling and contact with the divine that makes people love to read the Bible and claim that reading the Bible has changed their lives. The theological concepts, historical documentation, and all the rest won't, in and of themselves, deliver a spiritual experience or insight. Only when the mind makes its shift beyond the words does Spirit touch us.

This meditative approach to reading the Bible needs to be clarified, studied, and encouraged. I've read the Bible many times, and each time I've found myself approaching the experience more and more from this expectation of allowing the words I read to help shift my mind toward encountering Spirit. Often it does seem that the holy words are what provoke the Spirit encounter, but when looked at dispassionately, this doesn't seem to be the case. I say this because I can read other spiritual books from other religious cultures or even of contemporary authors and also be led into a state of mind in which thoughts fall away and Spirit inflows.

## When You Get the Message

I find that many people are actually addicted to the Bible as their only source of inspiration and contact with the divine. I hope you can see from what I've just written that this fixation on the Bible as the only path to Spirit inflow is limiting and not necessary – or even valid. One of my rancher father's favorite sayings was "When you get the message, hang up the phone." Spiritually, for me, this means that once the words of the Bible lead you to Spirit, you don't need to continue to fixate overmuch on the delivery vehicle.

> I recommend that you not become attached to reading the Bible (or any other book, including this one) as your one and only spiritual practice, or your only way to open to Spirit. Instead, begin to master the process for shifting from cognitive to intuitive-spiritual mode of consciousness in many different settings.

Anything, any experience that helps you quiet your thinking mind and tune in to your deeper intuitive and spiritual consciousness, should be nourished, cherished, and encouraged in your life. To accept the experience of Spirit inflow only in the context of traditional Christian formats not only limits your experience of Spirit severely, but is also a denial of the reality that Spirit is everywhere and in all things, and always ready to come to us in all contexts.

If the aim is to live in Spirit continually, then we need to let go of the written Word of God as our only access vehicle, and allow all of God's creation to encourage the inflow of Spirit.

## Whole-Body Holy Spirit

From the Gospels, we saw that the Holy Spirit comes to us not as a thought or idea, but as a whole-body experience. Jesus was "filled with the Holy Spirit." The Spirit of God touches the hearts of men – not just their minds. Certainly, when we're open to guidance, Spirit does touch our thoughts as well as our feelings and our actions, but there is always the sense that Spirit inflows into our whole physical being. Being touched by Spirit involves all our perceptions – we're engulfed in the experience.

> This means that, in order to encourage the inflow of Spirit into our lives, we need to learn to maintain regularly a whole-body state of awareness. We need to be present in the here and now, where Spirit lives, if we're going to experience the power, glory, and comfort of God's touch in our lives.

I'd like to begin teaching you the basic "whole-body" meditation that I teach in all my books, because it's the constant beginning place for opening to intuitive insight, heartfelt wisdom, and the touch of God. If you're not conscious of your whole-body presence, there's no way you can experience the touch of Spirit in your life – so the challenge is learning how. It's simple – move through this process as I describe it:

As you continue reading these words, expand your awareness so that you're also conscious of the sensation of the air flowing in and out of your nose as you breathe . . . turn your mind's attention toward the sensory world of the here and now . . . allow your awareness to expand naturally to include the air flowing in and out of your nose, and also the movements in your chest and belly as you breathe . . . and now expand your awareness to include the feelings in your heart, right in the middle of your breathing . . . And for the final expansion into whole-body awareness, allow your attention to expand to include your whole body at once, here in this present moment.

That's the most direct path to shifting from thoughts to present-moment awareness. Everywhere I go, I teach this process as a primal meditation. I strongly encourage you to begin to memorize the steps, and also go online to my site if you'd like my voice to guide you through the process over and over, until it becomes second nature to you to move regularly into this whole-body consciousness. Why? Because in this expanded state of awareness, Spirit naturally comes flowing into your personal bubble of awareness and transforms you into a conscious spiritual being.

#  Meditation Time

*Again, here are the four steps to this whole-body state of consciousness:*

1. Feel the air flowing in and out of your nose . . .

2. Also feel the movements in your chest and belly as you breathe . . .

3. At the same time, tune in to the feelings in your heart . . .

4. Expand to be aware of your whole body, here in this present moment . . .

Open your heart to a new experience!

# Pause & Experience

# 6

# From Belief . . . to Experience

As we saw in the last chapter, when we choose to manage our minds so that we live more and more in the present moment, we are choosing to live where God can contact us and live within and through us. My understanding of Jesus' deeper teaching is that the spiritual heart path leads us into a realm of consciousness where God does live vitally, even vivaciously, within our hearts, minds, and souls.

The one great power we have in life is our mental ability to shut God out of our consciousness. For me, this is psychologically the "great fall" experience that comes to most of us at some point in early childhood.

Very young children seem often to be living in the kingdom of heaven – they're radiant in the present moment, not lost in the past or the future, not judging, just being their natural spiritual selves. Jesus pointed this out clearly when he said that if we want to enter the kingdom of heaven, we must be as little children.

Then our minds develop the ability to create a concept of ourselves: an "ego identity" made up of personal experiences from the past merged with prevailing concepts and attitudes we've inherited from our culture. We become a distinct personality, a separate identity grounded in quite elaborate thoughts, attitudes, and beliefs about who we are and what life is all about.

This dominating ego function of the mind is actually essential to human survival; it assumes the essential task of overseer in making sure our individual identities and bodies continue to survive and flourish. Emerging from a competitive fear-based function of the mind, the ego "runs our show" by controlling the thoughts we think and the actions we take. Quite early on, it comes to believe that it's the center of the universe and that logical thought, life-planning, and action are primary gods to worship. The ego also tends to take on religious beliefs that serve its primary survival goals including, if possible, eternal life, so that survival is expected in the future to continue . . . forever.

As we get older and become more and more rooted in our ingrained attitudes and beliefs, we tend to avoid and ignore any new experiences that come to us that don't match our beliefs about who we are and what life is all about. Early on, we also become aware that if we don't manage our minds properly to fit into society, we could be considered crazy and locked up. So we shut out experiences that might be considered crazy (including deep spiritual experiences of a reality beyond the materialist reality our society accepts) and limit ourselves to thoughts and experiences that will be accepted.

As we grow up, our bubble of consciousness becomes less and less permeable. We avoid any threatening experiences or ideas. We filter out of our awareness – automatically, in most cases – inputs that would threaten or violate our beliefs and attitudes about what life is all about. And in this process, most of us end up shutting spiritual experience out of our everyday world.

This is very possibly what happened to you, if you find that opening your heart to the deeper spiritual mysteries of life isn't a natural everyday occurrence. If you're like most people, your ego shut unusual inner experiences out of mind, to the point that the very notion of opening to a greater consciousness than your ego consciousness might strike you as alien, threatening, or just downright silly. You might believe in God the Father, God the Son, and God the Holy Ghost as a lofty theological concept, but that doesn't mean your heart has remained open to experience the infinite radical spiritual reality behind such words.

> We live in a society that provides almost no reasonable psychological support and guidance for youngsters when they stumble into spiritual experience. They have to seek support in limiting fundamentalist beliefs or go it alone – or shut it out.

I hope that this book encourages a more reasonable alternative, where mature adults talk openly about spiritual experience, encourage it in their own lives in a balanced way, and offer support to youngsters as they open up and discover their spiritual identities.

## Beliefs and Emotions

Beliefs, by definition, are entirely past-oriented. All of our thoughts, ideas, and attitudes are likewise grounded in the past. Thought is a reflective process. In most cases, the mind cannot be lost in thought and focused on experience at the same time. That means we can't think about what is happening right now in this emerging moment. As soon as we shift into thinking about what's happening, we fixate on a recent memory, not a present experience. Thought is reflective – and what it reflects on is memory, even if that memory is just five seconds in the past. Therefore thoughts always take us away from the present moment and distance us from the experiential point at which Spirit enters our lives and dwells in our hearts.

All Christian theology is based on beliefs, which are ideas that live in the past/memory/intellect function of the mind. For instance, Christians believe that Christ died for their sins. *This belief is nothing more than an idea.* The idea can generate a host of emotional responses that move us deeply: Our thoughts have great power to evoke emotions. But the emotion is being stimulated by a cognitive process in the brain. We must be careful to differentiate between emotions generated by our thoughts, and inner feelings generated by direct experience.

**If you believe you're a hopeless sinner, then focusing on this thought will surely make you feel bad, guilty, and all the rest, right? If you believe that Jesus died for your sins, this belief will stimulate emotions such as guilt for causing someone's death, but also a liberating emotion at the thought that you've been eternally saved by his death.**

You might also dwell on your belief that Christ cares for you and helps you, and this thought will give you comfort. And as your associative mind moves from one belief to another, you might find yourself dwelling on your belief that you're never going to die, that you're going to go to heaven and live forever – and certainly this belief will lead to most wonderful feelings in your heart and body.

Therefore – because ideas and beliefs can stimulate good emotions in your body – believing the basic Christian theology can make you feel very good. This is the powerful impact of the Christian belief. It can make you feel good! As a child I lived within this belief system, and I often had absolutely blissful feelings when I thought about my beliefs.

But . . . doubts tormented me. What if my beliefs were wrong? What if the whole Christian thing wasn't true? Such doubts plague the religious life because beliefs are ultimately nothing more than hopeful ideas.

> We can base our lives on grand religious beliefs, but because we don't know directly if these beliefs are true, we live our lives plagued with doubt – which means we live in fear. To base our lives on beliefs is to choose to live in fear. To see this psychological reality is very important.

The unavoidable psychological fact is that to break free of fear, we must let go of our beliefs and turn our focus toward actually *experiencing* what is true in our lives. We must risk, we must leap, we must let go and have faith. We must say, "I'm tired of basing my life on religious ideas that I don't know are true or not. I want to let go of those *beliefs* and open up to *experience*, directly, what's true and real at the core of my existence."

At first, this seems dangerous and scary, to shift from belief to direct experience. But when you look closely at the situation, you'll find that the really scary thing is to remain locked in questionable ideas about spiritual reality, rather than opening up to knowing that reality directly. You'll never get beyond the anxiety of doubt until you tune in to the security of direct knowledge. This is certainly why Jesus said, "Know the truth, and the truth will set you free."

## Experience – The Eternal Present

Each moment, at the most basic level, we have a choice of two different ways of using our minds. We can be locked into our own thinking-imagining process in which thoughts and images flow through our minds based on how our ego chooses to manipulate and reconstruct the past. Or we can shift our focus toward the perceptual spontaneous present moment, where the flow of time disappears.

Physical perceptual reality is, of course, purely a present-moment affair. There is no tangible future – we might conjure up a snazzy image of what might happen in the future, but it remains nothing more than a mental construct. The same with the past – we can store in memory experiences we've had of the past, but when we remember those memories, we recreate them in the present moment. Even memory happens in the here and now. Philosophers have mulled over this truth for eons and they always come to the same conclusion, even though it contradicts our everyday assumptions.

It's obvious that if there's really no past or future except in our brain's imagination and memory banks, the only place we'll actually experience Spirit and God is in the present moment.

> Going back in our minds two thousand years ago in history isn't where we'll encounter the living presence of Jesus. Thinking forward to heaven isn't where we'll encounter God. Only right here, right now, will we ever experience spiritual reality.

But curiously, there's a great safety in living in beliefs and imaginings. Many people are scared to death of the possibility of a direct encounter with God. It's safe to live within belief systems that are forever frozen in our minds as secure places we can go that generate nice comfy emotions in our hearts when we dwell on the beliefs. This is, in my opinion, a spiritual addiction. We stimulate good feelings but avoid reality. We dwell within our mind's religious creation rather than allowing the reality of Spirit to indwell.

> In this sense, all religious beliefs are idols. For thousands of years, the priestly cult has encouraged people to worship belief structures, rather than worshipping only the reality of the Creator. How is it that such a thing has happened, when the Bible says clearly not to worship idols?

I know at least part of the answer. The feelings in our hearts evoked by worshipping our thought-creations fool us into believing that we're in touch with the real thing. And there's always the priestly fear factor, saying that if you let go of your beliefs something seriously terrible will happen to you.

This is the nature of the priestly cult's fear-based manipulation of the human populace, and it needs a bright light focused on it until all people see it clearly. Certainly, most priests, ministers, and pastors are simply caught up in the same beliefs, not consciously manipulating the populace. But the underlying structure of traditional religious belief systems is almost always grounded in a fear-based, false-hope theology.

## Know the Truth

What to do? Just make the choice. Decide that you want to open up and experience what's real, rather than living inside questionable beliefs and uncertain hopes. And how to accomplish this opening up? First of all, observe right to the core the logical fact that all beliefs are rooted in abstract thought. As soon as you quiet such thoughts and focus your mind's attention devotedly on the present moment, you can shift yourself away from the dominance of the past, of beliefs, and awaken your engagement with the emerging present moment.

> Right here, right now, with no further hesitation, you are in position to experience the truth of life. This is it. If you honestly look to discover what is true spiritually, beyond all beliefs, this truth will come to you. As Jesus promised, "Ask and it will be given to you. Seek and you will find. Knock and it will open up to you."

The inflow of Holy Spirit is always an experience. And because we can never have the same experience twice (by the very nature of the flow of organic planetary time), our spiritual experience will always be new. Please don't think that every time you open to Spirit you'll experience the same thing. Just the opposite – you'll never experience Spirit in the same way twice.

This is very important. You simply cannot form a valid concept of what spiritual insight is, based on past experience, because the next time you open to Spirit and have this experience, it's going to be new! That's what it means to live in the eternal moment: It's infinite, it's always emerging, and it's always surprising. That's how God set up this universe, so that's how we experience life. Always new, each new moment.

And that's exactly why *beliefs distance us from God* – because beliefs become rigid and stuck in past experience and expectations, while each new moment moves into a new reality, a new expression of God's presence in our lives.

> To choose to live within a belief system is to choose to drift deeper and deeper into a past that doesn't even exist except in our own minds. To choose to live in the always-emerging experience of the present moment is to remain in intimate communion with God's creation and presence, here and now.

Jesus stated this truth in many ways. He told us, "The kingdom of heaven is at hand," right here, not in the future. He told us that only with the mental openness and spontaneity of little children can we enter the kingdom of heaven. He told us to consider the lilies, who attain their remarkable beauty without ever once thinking or planning about the future. He told us not to worry about what we will say in difficult situations, but rather to trust that the deeper wisdom and power of Spirit will act through us if we stay centered in the present moment.

Therefore when I read in the Bible certain quotes assigned to Jesus that push me into thinking about beliefs and theological imaginations, I suspect I'm reading words that were put in Jesus' mouth. But when I read words attributed to Jesus that encourage genuine present-moment spiritual awareness and spontaneous heart-centered behavior, I know I'm reading the real thing, and I take these sayings deeply to heart.

# 🌱 Experience Time

*Let's do it again – take a mind break in which you can allow these words you're reading to shift your mind's awareness toward present-moment sensations and experiences. Meditation is all about turning your attention toward the present moment, as you allow your consciousness to expand to include more and more of God's immediate "here and now" creation. Ultimately, in meditation, you'll find that your beliefs fall entirely away and your consciousness expands infinitely, so that you and God are experienced as truly one – that's the ultimate spiritual experience, as far as I can see. That's what meditation is all about: Embracing the experience of the present moment so that you let go of your limited ego identity, and experience a greater sense of who you are as you merge with Spirit, and become whole.*

*So . . . as you read these words, and as a process to learn to do on your own, begin to expand your awareness to include the sensations in your nose as the air flows in . . . and flows out . . . and in again . . . and now expand your awareness to include also the movements in your chest and belly as you breathe . . . and when you're ready, also begin to be aware of the feelings in your heart right now . . . and expand your awareness to include your whole body, here in this present moment . . . also tune in to the sounds around you . . . the sense of volume and depth of the space around you . . . the scents in the air . . . the gentle pressure of the air on your skin . . . the pull of gravity holding you to the earth . . . just breathe into this full experience . . . and say to yourself, "my heart is open to new experience . . ." and as you breathe into this new moment, see what new experience comes to you . . .*

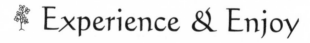 🌿 Experience & Enjoy

# 7

# From Life Hereafter . . . to the Eternal Now

Much of the everlasting Christian allure has surely been its promise that we don't ever have to die if we accept Christ as our savior. That's the best sales pitch the world has ever heard – almost everyone is afraid of facing their mortal demise. And who wouldn't give a great deal to be able somehow to avoid death altogether?

Naturally, in order to promise eternal escape from personal annihilation, there must be someplace that we go after our physical bodies cease to exist. In this light, I found it curious at seminary to discover that traditional pre-Christian Judaism made very little mention of a celestial hereafter.

**The belief in an otherworldly perfect place in the sky**

> where true believers go after their physical death seems to
> have come into being historically around the time of Jesus,
> and matured half a century later.

From an anthropological point of view, early human beings seem to have developed their mental ability to remember the past long, long before they began to develop the ability to project an imagined leap into the future. The past can be said to exist because we personally can remember what happened "in the past." But the future is far more ephemeral – none of us has experienced the future, except in our imaginations. As far as I have investigated, only around the time of Jesus did this new driving passion about the fate of our individual souls in the future come into being in the world, beginning with the quite innovative Greek philosophers, then the somewhat copycat Roman philosophers, then Christian philosophers.

> It was long in coming, but once the idea of heaven began
> to take root in human minds, a wildfire was set upon the
> world – a passion for eternal life that is still consuming
> human hearts with the agonizing hope that perhaps we
> don't have to die as ego-entities, after all.

Even in the earliest documents of the preaching of the disciples after Jesus' death, the final punch line following the sin-guilt-salvation routine was the promise that if we give our souls totally to Christ as our Lord and Savior, not only do we escape our sinful nature, we also receive the eternal blessing of living in our personal ego-bubble forever.

It's perhaps important to note that, six hundred years after Jesus, Christian communities were still springing up and in many cases flourishing throughout the Near East. Even in the Arab city of Mecca, there was a respected Christian community and school that Mohammed historically visited and probably even studied at. And as Mohammed (a new prophet in the lineage of Moses, Abraham, and Jesus) began to establish his new religion, he very clearly established the existence and ready access to a perfect heaven in the sky, his religion's central attraction. He even outdid the Christians by throwing in an overload of young virgins in the bargain.

In earlier religions such as Taoism, Hinduism, and Buddhism, a dimension of eternal life was definitely offered, and also experienced. But the Eastern approach to attaining eternal life was through a process of meditation in which practitioners let go of their finite earthly ego identities and merged their experiential souls with the infinite divine. Christianity offered something radically new: the hope that you could take your ego with you when you died, and continue to enjoy your individual ego identity in heaven, just as on Earth.

Why has this offer of eternal life of the ego so dominated the Christian and Moslem theology – and why has this offer made these two relatively new religions the most popular and expanding religions on the face of the earth? What is it about death of the mortal body and the psychological ego that scares us so much that we'll sell our souls to whoever can convince us that they have a way to avoid mortal death?

## Facing Death – Unafraid?

One of the basic truths of being born a mortal human being on this planet is that no one gets out of here alive. We have our beginning in the womb and we have our ending in the grave – or wherever. Our life is a finite linear progression whether we like it or not. These bodies of ours have a built-in termination code. If everyone lived forever, the planet would become so overpopulated that it would be the end for everyone.

> For the sake of new generations, we old farts need to accept that we've lived a full life, and then get out of the way. That's what mortal planetary existence is all about. You live a long full life, if you're lucky, and then you die and make room for the next batch of kids.

Mortality is fine for animals that don't have an advanced quality of consciousness that can imagine they might somehow continue indefinitely into the future. Consciousness is a mysterious wonderful thing in that we are able to tap into levels of reality that transcend the physical. In meditation or even during moments of sudden spontaneous realization, we can suddenly plug in to a greater consciousness than our personal ego awareness. And once we've experienced that we are somehow "more" than the reach of our physical senses, our minds, of course, begin reflecting and imagining just what this "more" might consist of.

As mentioned earlier, long before Jesus and Mohammed brought the belief of a heavenly future into prominence in the world, both the Taoist tradition in China and the Hindu and Buddhist traditions in southern Asia taught that through meditation we can indeed become one with God and merge our personal consciousness with the Infinite Consciousness.

**But curiously, those great Eastern traditions did not establish a belief in a personal Godhead. They didn't develop a faith based on a personal relationship with a God who seemed to be a human being just like us, with all our emotions and thoughts raised to an infinite level of expression.**

Instead, those ancient religions offered a differing belief, and most notably a belief that could be substantiated through direct inner encounter in meditation with the primal reality of the universe. This meditative path enabled people to transcend mortal death by experiencing the existence in the present moment of a union between our personal consciousness and the Infinite Consciousness.

Christianity and Islam went a radical step further with their promises, and became so successful, at least in part, because they offered our egos something more than just a general experience of oneness with the divine. Christianity and Islam offered, and still continue to promise loudly, the existence of a very personal God who relates with us man to man (or male God to female person) and personally welcomes not only our spiritual soul, but also our ego personality into the eternal embrace of heavenly bliss.

This promise is absolutely great – except there's one hitch. On close examination of this promise, we find that the promise is based on nothing more than the following: a completely untested and intrinsically unverifiable belief involving future possibilities that we can't verify as right or wrong until after we die. And then, well – whatever we get, we get. The future doesn't even exist until it becomes the present moment, so there's just no way of knowing what's going to happen.

> So even though we might fervently hope that our personal psychological identities continue after we die, there's no assurance that this is true. So with our fervent hope of an afterlife comes the nagging doubt that the belief isn't true – and with this doubt comes an existential anxiety that seriously corrupts the Christian soul.

In opposite direction to a future heavenly pie in the sky, Jesus very often taught that the present moment is where Spirit is to be found and where the kingdom of heaven is happening – not somewhere off in the future. "The kingdom of heaven is at hand," as mentioned earlier, is a clear indication to focus on the present moment rather than the future. Yes, I know that Jesus was also quoted as promising to go and prepare a place for us in heaven. But in my unorthodox approach to the Gospels, when I find such totally contradictory teachings of Jesus in the Bible, I assume that I have the spiritual right in meditation to explore which of the teachings ring true and which seem added to support a particular religious theology.

My reading of the Gospels and, much more important, my experience in meditation and life in general tell me that, first of all, Jesus reached a point where he didn't fear his mortal death.

My understanding of this is that he most definitely, as a highly advanced spiritual being, was continually in an expanded state of consciousness in which he was one with God, in the eternal present moment.

He knew from direct experience, as can we all, that we are greater than our ego thinks we are. He knew that even though his body would naturally at some point cease to exist, his deeper consciousness that was eternally one with God would somehow continue. So where, death, is thy sting?

> I feel that one of the deepest lessons we can learn from tuning in to the living presence of Jesus is that we don't have to be afraid of death. There is no way of knowing what happens when we die – that's the future. But in the very act of communing with Jesus in meditation, we experience directly that we are right here, right now, existing in an eternal present moment that lies outside our mortal linear flow of life-death time.

For me, this is the reasonable, realistic solution to our fear of death. Yes, we're going to die and enter into a nonphysical consciousness. No, we can't trust any promises that we're going to go to a heaven of our own imagining. But yes, we can experience, directly in meditation and communion with God, our eternal spiritual nature.

And finally, yes, our ego needs to come to grips with the psychological reality that its entire mental construct of a personal identity based on past personal events is going to cease to exist or go through some transformation that, quite honestly, no one can imagine – because it's beyond the realm of physical experience on which all our imagining is based.

> It's a perfect two-hundred-percent situation, a paradox like most spiritual situations. Yes, we are going to depart earthly linear time and at that biological level cease to exist. And yes, we are even right now conscious and par-

ticipating in the eternal present moment that does not cease to exist.

We do best to focus our attention here in the present moment and live fully in this heaven on Earth we've been blessed with. Worrying about the future, or imagining the future, is holding our attention on a realm that doesn't even exist. Fixating on the future is a waste of precious spiritual time.

## Jesus' Presence Here and Now

I'd like to share with you a private feeling and experience that underlies all I have to say in this book. After getting kicked out of the Christian Church for questioning the priestly cult's dictums overmuch, and also for meditating overmuch, I spent a lot of time off in non-Christian realms, exploring the depths of Taoist, Zen, Hindu, and Buddhist meditative experience. I will always be thankful for what I learned in those non-Western approaches to God.

At a certain point, however, as mentioned earlier, I suddenly realized that when I opened my heart to communion with God in meditation or otherwise, I continued to sense the presence of Jesus. For a while, my heart and mind were closed to this personal presence, but then I finally realized that my negative attitude toward all things Christian was shutting me off from a reality that transcended theology and church doctrine.

I opened up again and, indeed, the presence of Jesus as a spiritual mentor, guide, comforter, and all the rest awakened a depth of spiritual experience in me that I simply wasn't attaining while meditating in a Buddhist or Zen mind-state. I had sometimes felt the personal presence of Buddha in my meditations, but this was not my tradition, and somehow when I opened to Jesus' spiritual presence, something deeper happened.

So I can clearly say, there is a special power and grace, at least for me, in opening my heart to the highest (if I can say that nonjudgmentally) personal spiritual presence of my own tradition. Otherwise, I wouldn't be writing this book at all.

> We do, at least sometimes, need guidance and support from the highest human link we can find to God Almighty. Jesus is very much that link for me. Maria Magdalena is equally that link when I need a more feminine quality in my meditations. And certainly, the Holy Spirit is the dominant spiritual presence throughout.

Perhaps we should reflect a few moments on these different qualities of the traditional Christian Trinity and how they can evolve into a new vision of the multiple ways by which we can link with the divine.

## The New Trinity

First of all, God the Father is an expression from traditional Jewish theology. The Israelites were extremely paternalistic, as were all the Arab tribes of the Near East – and so they mostly remain. I certainly don't see God as a father figure. This is obviously anthropomorphic and of a low religious level of belief. The Creator of this entire universe (and probably multiple universes) is far beyond the sexual duality on which just a part of reproduction on this planet is based. So for me, the first part of the New Trinity is God the Creator, not God the Father.

We can, in meditation and at any moment in our lives, tune directly in to this infinite spiritual creative presence. Sometimes I still tap feelings of God as a father figure and I accept these feelings. After all, when I was little, I experienced my father as God in some ways. But certainly, as an adult, I don't build a theology around God as sexually male.

At a more personal human level, we can also focus on a spiritual presence that was once an individual human being and, through this more personal contact, we can enter into a special quality of spiritual awakening. For me, this is through Jesus and

Maria Magdalena. The two of them together represent for me what was traditionally called God the Son. I want to expand this second part of the New Trinity, however, to include all totally awakened spiritual beings who lived on this Earth at some point and after physical death continue to be there for us when we open up and ask for guidance and help.

Many people seek a very personal emotional feeling and sense of intimate relationship with these spiritual/human links to God, as if to bypass human relationships. I personally don't push anymore for such an overly personal emotional contact during meditation.

The human emotions are preprogrammed biochemical hormonal responses of our physical bodies to various situations. And I feel that the experience of spiritual communion is somehow quite different from the emotions of intimacy and closeness that we experience in sexual bonding and human-to-human relating. My opinion is that we should seek human emotions with our fellow humans.

In meditation, there's a purification of our quality of emotions. The relationship between our mortal hearts and the infinite spiritual divine first heals our emotional traumas and hungers, then shifts us into a quality of peace, love, acceptance, and knowing that is beyond our animal emotional reactions – that is, in fact, the peace that transcends all human understanding.

The third part of the New Trinity is of course the Holy Spirit. I must say, this quality of the Trinity is where I tend to focus my meditative attention most often. When I'm in extreme emotions or soul-searching, I do open to Jesus and Magdalena's presence, guidance, and support.

But usually, I hunger for that beautiful but nonemotional feeling of the inflow of Spirit and love into my heart, my mind, and my life. Jesus brought Spirit and love into the hearts of his followers. And nurturing this inflow, for me, is the true spiritual intent.

So yes, there remains a sense of the Trinity in this post-Christian approach to spiritual living. The bottom line of the Trinity connects Jesus and Magdalena with Holy Spirit as our human base of spiritual relating. And each of the lines rising up to the high point of God the Creator links us with the infinite divine. Each time we enter into meditation, we never know at what level we're going to spontaneously encounter the Trinity. That's what makes meditation so exciting – we are naturally guided and led each time into a unique experience of our relationship with God.

## Not My Will, but Thine

It's vital to realize that it's our ego mind that is afraid of our impending death. Very possibly (although I'm not at all certain either way), our accumulated personality based on past experiences of this lifetime will indeed fade into nothingness when we die physically. And the ego will certainly go if our personality goes – so of course, death scares our ego to death!

But throughout my recent writings, I've been exploring the observable fact that our ego has the capacity to learn, grow, and come to understand its own ground of being. I feel that my ego is now integrated into my deeper spiritual sense of who I am, and has come to accept, quite without fear, the possibility of its own demise.

> This is one of the great natural gifs of meditating regularly: Your ego does mature and let go, step by step, of its earlier fears. And as your ego lets go of its preprogrammed biological fears, it becomes an integral part of your spiritual process, doing its part to point your mind's attention steadily in highly worthwhile directions.

Ultimately, we are always choosing to focus on things that make us react with fear and aggression, or on things that make us respond with love and cooperation. Once we let go of fear-based beliefs and fixations and open ourselves to living in the eternal present moment – once we let go of the manipulation, let go of the self-centered attitudes and future-based strivings, and instead surrender to a greater guidance in our lives – we attain a greater power in our actions.

This choice is between being dominated by our animal will or our higher will. Jesus said it perfectly in regard to his own relationship with God: "Not my will, but thine." We can either run our lives based on our animal reactions and selfish motivations, or surrender our lives to the guidance of the Greater Intelligence of the universe.

Once we see the choice, of course, there's no choice. Who would want to risk running their lives with seriously limited ego intelligence and perspective when there's a greater consciousness we can tap into that sees the whole, understands the larger vision, and guides us toward a more fulfilling experience of life? Who would want to live a life based on fear and greed when we can live our lives based on love and faith? Given the choice, who would want to place their bet on the ego function of the mind versus the higher spiritual function of the mind?

But it doesn't even come down to that either-or. As I mentioned before, what's amazing is that when we open our hearts to allow the higher will to express itself through us, our ego isn't thrown out, it's transformed. There's no loss of ego function when Spirit acts through us. The ego is actually more than eager, when it experiences the guidance of Spirit, to surrender to the higher guidance and wisdom.

> Our minds are continually evaluating our moment-to-moment situation and making decisions on what best to do next. All that happens when we open up to Spirit in our lives is that those decisions begin to be guided by a higher wisdom and power. You can call it intuitive insight if you don't want to mention Spirit. It's ultimately all the same.

For me, there's no real division between our minds' higher intuitive function and our functioning when we merge our individual consciousness with the Greater Consciousness. In my business books, I don't even mention the word "Spirit," because when we open our hearts and minds to the higher intuitive function of the human mind and feel connected with our inner source of being, we naturally expand into whatever that "spiritual" experience might be called. Our higher self is in natural communion with the infinite intelligence of the universe. Call it God, call it insight, call it wisdom or whatever – it's real. And we can surrender our ego will to that greater will, and thrive!

> What's important is developing a regular meditative practice in which we learn to manage our minds so that we do open up to our higher selves, to spiritual guidance, to the touch of God in our lives. That's what we're going to explore and learn how to do in the rest of this book.

I thank you for moving perhaps quite bravely through this first part of the book. I know that, for many of you, it's been somewhat touchy yet absolutely essential to expose and re-evaluate old beliefs and attitudes you were perhaps programmed with, so that you can begin to choose to let go of beliefs that don't serve you, and embrace a more realistic, experientially true approach to your inner life. Please return to these discussions, and also join us online for further guided experience and forum discussions of these seven essential themes.

For the rest of this book, it's time to become more specific in identifying the teachings of Jesus that point directly toward a meditative path that will bring us into regular communion with God by whatever name. The challenge is to learn how to open our hearts to the inflow of love and the guidance of our higher being and, by extension, the total intelligence, compassion, and wisdom of the Creator of our universe and beyond . . .

# ✣ Reflection Time

*Let's move through one of the audio-guided sessions you'll find online (www.johnselby.com). You can also read through this right now, take in each new suggestion, and breathe into its power to evoke experience and insight within you.*

*Feel free to relax . . . let go of tensions . . . stretch and yawn a bit if you want to . . . settle into a comfortable position . . . tune in to the sensation of the air flowing in and out of your nose . . . and the movements in your chest and belly . . . also be aware of the feelings in your heart . . . and your whole-body presence right here, right now . . .*

*Notice what experience comes to you when you say each of the following statements in turn, and breathe for a few moments into the feelings and insights that arise:*

*"I let go of ideal Christ images . . . and open up to Jesus' presence."*

*"I quiet my thoughts . . . and open up to feelings in my heart."*

*"I let go of being a sinner . . . and open up to forgiveness and love."*

*"I let go of scriptures . . . and open to inspiration – right now."*

*"I let go of my beliefs . . . and open up to spiritual experience."*

*"I let go of dreams of the future . . . and open to eternal life – right now."*

*And now let all words go . . . and breathe into a new experience . . .*

#  Pause & Experience

# Part Two

# Living the New Relationship

In the second part of this book, I'd like to explore with you a qualitatively new sense of spiritual relationship, which opens up with Jesus in the present moment when we focus on certain very powerful words that Jesus is quoted as saying – words that very directly help awaken Spirit in our lives right here, right now.

Jesus stated that his intent was not to destroy the law, but to fulfill it. He wanted to show us how to break free from religious strictures and know the truth directly. In his teachings, he offered several new commandments that radically transform our relationship with God. Yet it seems that, after two thousand years, his true spiritual message has rarely been clearly heard or acted on. In this section, we'll consider in depth seven primary uplifting commandments that Jesus gave us. When taken as a whole, they point the way clearly toward a new direct relationship with the divine in which we attain heaven here in this present moment.

# 8

# "Fear not . . . judge not"

Jesus seems to have said very little about what we should *avoid* doing in life. In fact, throughout the four Gospels, there are only two dramatic statements he's quoted as saying, loud and clear, that carry a negative intonation. They also happen to be the most insightful commandments ever to ring in human ears. They stand as our primary psychological challenge if we're to walk the path Jesus walked.

In my studies of theology, church history, and all the rest when I was at seminary, I approached Christian doctrine primarily from the point of view of a psychologist. I'd already completed most of my psychological studies before going to seminary, so naturally, I tended to look at the teachings in the Bible with a primary question in mind: Does what I'm reading make rational as well as spiritual sense, knowing what I do about how the mind works and how human beings function?

In this first chapter, we're going to look to the heart of Jesus' psychological genius by considering those two negative orders he laid down like massive foundation stones to support our heart path. In their power and wisdom, we'll discover the entire scope of psychological healing – and also the most direct path to spiritual awakening.

It's amazing that Jesus needed only four words to encapsulate the entire tradition of Western therapy and psychology. With these four words, he identified and neutralized the two functions of the human mind that cause 90 percent of our emotional suffering, physical conflict, and general mental confusion and despair. We're talking, of course, about fear and judgment. These two cognitive functions of the mind are responsible for almost all of our negative thoughts, attitudes, emotions, and actions.

Fear-based thoughts underlie all our worries, hostilities, tensions, and aggressions. And the judgmental function of the mind works hand in hand with the fear function of the mind, generating negative reactions, emotions, and actions.

Psychologists have now realized that all aggression and anger have their origin in a fear reaction. Almost always, if you aren't threatened, you won't be aggressive. And if you're not afraid, you won't get up the steam to feel angry – because anger emerges directly out of fear.

As long as we let our minds run mostly on automatic, we tend to get stuck in worried thoughts, in negative judgments, in chronic fear-based contraction from the world. Jesus clearly saw this basic human dynamic and stated right up front, just don't do it! Judge not. Fear not. End of discussion.

## Beyond Fear – Into Love

Of course, letting go of fear and judgment is easier said than done – or is it? Almost all of my work as a therapist was focused on helping people learn how to shift their attention away from chronic fear-based judgmental thoughts and imaginings toward more productive inner experiences. I used to employ a battery of complicated therapy techniques for helping people work slowly through their childhood fears and programmed judgments. But at a certain point, I realized that the utter simplicity of Jesus' brief commandments, "Fear not – judge not," carried a remarkably simple solution within the format of the declaration.

It's important to note that Jesus didn't play therapist with his followers and spend years helping them work out all their negative fearful mental patterns. Instead, he gave them the clear order simply to take charge of their minds and stop fixating on those patterns – right now!

Once I realized this, I spent a decade wearing my psychologist's hat, researching how the mind can actually shift, right now, away from the fear-judgment function of the brain toward more compassionate, expansive functions of the mind. For a number of years, this basic "cognitive shifting" process seemed to elude me. But then suddenly – in meditation, not while cogitating or doing research! – I saw the light.

Given proper cognitive tools, you have the power each moment to shift out of fear and judgment. This is actually not difficult to do – you simply need to understand that you have the choice, right now, of continuing to fixate on inner thoughts and imaginings that are fearful and judgmental, or to turn your attention to thoughts and experiences that are trusting and accepting.

What enabled me to suddenly see a path beyond fear and judgment was realizing that Jesus didn't just lay down his two negative commandments and walk away. He also told us positively where best to focus our mind's power of attention. He said, "Love one another, as I have loved you."

Being the remarkable psychologist that he was, Jesus knew that we *can't* be fixated on fear and judgment and focused on love and trust at the same time. In any given moment, we're either stuck in worried, aggressive, tormented thoughts, or we're focused on acceptance and love. His primary commandment was to focus on acceptance and love.

With his bold commandment "Fear not," Jesus wasn't demanding that we do something psychologically impossible. He was pointing out that we always have the choice (if we learn how to make it) of focusing our attention on fear, or love. When we talk about walking the heart path, that's exactly what we're talking about: choosing each moment where to focus our minds' attention.

## Cognitive Shifting Secrets

When you read the Gospels, you'll notice that much of what Jesus was teaching concerned where we choose to focus our mind's power of attention. When he said, "Consider the lilies," he was turning our attention to experience those lilies. When he said, "The kingdom of heaven is at hand," he was pointing to the exact place we can focus our attention in order to enter the kingdom of heaven.

And when he said, "Fear not – judge not – love one another," he was clearly indicating that we are to shift our focus away from mental thoughts and images that generate fear and judgment toward the center of love in our own bodies – our hearts.

At any given moment, most of our attention is devoted to focusing either on the past and the future (thinking, imagining, plotting, remembering, worrying, and all the rest) or on the present moment (sensing, feeling, and relating). When fear is closely examined, we find that it's almost always a past-future process in the mind. Unless we're physically threatened by a lion, a truck, or a bully in the present moment, our anxieties are all about what might happen in the future, based on bad things that have happened in the past.

Worrying is clearly a past-future fixation. Conversely, love is something we feel in our hearts in the present moment. Anxiety is provoked by thoughts inside our minds. Love is an experience that comes to us as a whole-body feeling right here, right now.

This means that if you want to follow Jesus' driving suggestion to stop being caught up in fear, you need to learn how to shift your focus away from thoughts about the past and the future, toward your experience right now in your heart. It's the same with judgment. Judgment is entirely a product of the thinking mind as it projects its own attitudes, judgments, and stereotypes on a person or a situation. Judgment is an associative thought that yanks you out of direct participation in the present moment and separates you from whatever you're encountering.

Of course, we do need to keep discriminating between red lights and green lights. I'm sure Jesus wasn't talking about simple discrimination when he said, "Judge not." He was talking about our chronic habit of categorizing everything we encounter, of stuffing people and events into cubbyholes based on past experience, rather than opening up to a unique new experience in the present moment. In this light, he talked about how we need to have the minds of little children to enter the kingdom of heaven, that is, be so much in the present moment that we don't get sucked off into judgment or fear mode by everything we encounter.

## Awareness to the Fore

If you often find that you're worrying, that you're judging, that you're stuck in negative thoughts that pull you out of the kingdom of heaven in the here and now, what can you do to follow Jesus' commandments to let go of judgments and worries? The first step is simply to become more aware of the thoughts you allow to run through your mind all the time.

Watch your habitual thoughts. Catch yourself, over and

over, mulling about negative things that have happened in the past or that you fear might happen in the future. And realize deeply that these thoughts are the source of most of your anxiety and stress.

In other words, you're torturing yourself. No one else is forcing you to think thoughts that make you tense with apprehension or growl with judgment. And inherent in Jesus' challenge to stop judging and worrying is the underlying commandment to take charge of your thoughts. This is surely one of the primal spiritual acts a human being can learn to take.

A great deal of the priestly manipulatory strategy throughout all cultures and all ages has depended on making people feel they have no power over what happens to them. By declaring in doctrinal statements that you are born a hopeless sinner, theologians declared that you are a helpless victim. Your animal nature will inevitably drag you down and there's nothing you can do about it – except buy into the priestly game of selling your soul in exchange for some force or power outside you saving you from your own nature.

Psychologically, this victim mentality of Christian doctrine simply isn't a true understanding of our mental potential. As cognitive science is proving more and more, we do have the inner power to take charge of our own minds, to quiet thoughts that are negative and self-damaging, and focus on thoughts and experiences that lift us up and make us whole.

So I would like to challenge you, specifically, to begin to observe your thoughts as they go through your mind. At first, don't try to change them at all. Just focus on your breathing . . . and at the same time, observe what thoughts begin to run through your mind. When you're at work, commuting, going for a walk, brushing your teeth, taking a shower, making love, whatever, stay aware of what's actually happening inside your mind. This is the first step to freeing yourself from mental habits that don't serve you.

And note this: Fear causes consciousness to contract. When you're anxious, your awareness collapses. Judgment does the same; your awareness drops down to a cognitive function of the mind that shuts out new experience and locks you in past-comparison thinking. Conversely, when you accept and love people and your situation without judgment or anxiety, your consciousness expands beautifully. You experience more fully, and allow the higher intuitive and spiritual functions of the mind to engage. And again – *you* are always making the choice, based on how you manage your mind, on whether you're operating with contracted reduced awareness or expanded awareness.

## Letting Fear and Judgment Go

You are a victim of your own mental habits and cultural programming – until you realize that you have the power to focus your mind's power of attention wherever you choose. That's the primal ego function of the mind: aiming your attention in the most important direction each new moment. If you're like most people, you developed defensive mental habits early in childhood. You worry about what might happen, and you problem-solve in an attempt to manipulate your life to avoid all the dangers that might befall you.

> Up to a point, this defensive stance is perhaps necessary. But when judgments and worrying dominate your thoughts and, in turn, provoke upsetting emotions that undermine not only your fun, but also your health and your spiritual growth, it's time to take charge of your mind, and consciously refocus your attention in directions that better serve you.

And as I said before, it's actually quite simple to do this, once you realize the vital importance of cognitive shifting – from being fixated on the past and the future (stuck in thought) to focusing more on the present moment (tuning in to experience). When you're lost in thought, you're basically gone from your body and the present moment. When you choose to focus on your body experience in the here and now, you pop back into the present moment. Upsetting thoughts become quiet, and you re-enter the kingdom of heaven. The beginning part of the meditation you'll learn in the final section of this book teaches you how to accomplish this cognitive-shifting process. Here's a beginning taste of that shifting process.

# 🌿 Reflection Time

*Gently turn your attention (even while reading these words) to include the present-moment experience of the air flowing in and out of your nose . . . actually feel the sensation of the air rushing in and out . . . tune in to your very essence of being a living creature breathing the earth's atmosphere – here you are!*

*Now move even deeper into the present moment, by also being aware of the movements in your chest and belly as you breathe . . . expand your mind's experience so that you tune in to the volume inside your chest and belly that expands and contracts with each breath . . . and right in the middle of that present-moment experience, also be aware of the feelings you find in your heart right now as you breathe . . .*

*Now explore what happens inside your mind and body when you say to yourself, "I let go of my worries and judgments . . . and open my heart to love." Say this statement of intent over and over . . . and allow these words to awaken inner experiences . . . allow your awareness to expand into whatever the present moment brings you right now . . .*

 **Pause & Experience**

# 9

# "Consider the lilies, and how they grow"

It seems that two thousand years ago, people were busy managing (or mismanaging) their minds in ways similar to those we use today. Over and over, Jesus noticed that his followers were caught up in worries about the future – and over and over, he found ways of suggesting a different way of moving through each new day. Often he used nature as a positive example. In this light, his teachings point toward a mystical and, at the same time, utterly pragmatic vision in which nature itself, God's perfect creation, shows us how to live our lives.

As I showed in detail in *Seven Masters, One Path,* Jesus taught an approach to life very similar to that taught by the ancient Chinese Taoist master Lao Tzu. For both of them, there was little point in scheming and manipulating one's way through life.

Instead, Jesus and Lao Tzu taught that there is a dramatically different way to survive and even thrive in the world,
and this way can be observed directly in nature, by contem-
plating the effortless yet successful "thoughtless" lives of
plants and animals.

Consider the lilies . . . these flowers fulfill their nature without
thought, without worry, without stress or effort at all. They are
totally here and now. Similarly, Jesus suggests that when we live
fully in the present moment, when we let go of judgment and
fear and allow the life force and Spirit to fill our lives, we thrive
like the lilies – we flourish naturally and joyfully.

Here is the direct quote from the Gospels so you can see
exactly what Jesus has to say about all this: "Consider the lilies,
and how they grow; they neither toil nor spin; yet I tell you, even
Solomon in all his glory was not arrayed like one of these. If God
so clothes the grass which is alive in the field today and tomorrow
is thrown into the oven, how much more will he clothe you?"

For quite some years (especially since I came of age in the
late sixties when the hippie philosophy was strong in the air), I
struggled to understand this saying. Was Jesus actually recommending that we stop being responsible for our own well-being,
quit our jobs, and sit around waiting for God to miraculously take
care of us? He said the same thing about animals: "Consider also
the ravens: they neither sow nor reap, they have neither store-
house nor barn, and yet God feeds them. Of how much more
value are you than the birds!"

In my current understanding, Jesus is pointing toward a special trusting relationship with God's creation in which we stop
assuming that we must manipulate the world around us to give us
what we need to survive. Instead, without worrying, we can fully
participate in the emerging present moment, as the plants and
animals do, and cooperate in a greater plan that will sustain us.

In the very next verse, Jesus goes on to finish expressing this
new vision by asking: "Which of you by being anxious can

add a cubit to his span of life? If you are not able to do as small a thing as that, why are you anxious about the rest?"

Here we have the heart of the matter: Jesus talking directly about anxiety, about worrying about our future, and pointing out that worrying doesn't do us a bit of good. He then goes on and concludes with his general "Fear not" dictum, said slightly anew: "Don't worry about what you are going to eat or drink, nor be of anxious mind. For all the nations of the world seek these things; and your Father knows that you need them. Instead, seek his kingdom, and these things shall be yours as well."

Again, there's a definite psychological logic to Jesus' teachings, which is so often overlooked. He not only tells you not to focus on your fears and worries – he also tells you specifically where to focus.

"Instead, seek his kingdom, and these things shall be yours as well." I consider this one of the primary gems of Jesus' teachings. He's telling us precisely how to manage our minds. He assures us that God knows what we need already, that we don't need to fixate chronically on our worries. Instead, we need to shift our focus to the power and glory of the eternal present moment.

"Fear not," he says, yet again, "for it is your Father's good pleasure to give you the kingdom." This is a very unusual saying – Jesus speaking of what gives God pleasure. Here we have the secret to trusting life and living like the lilies, without struggle, worry, or stress: God actually takes pleasure in giving us what we need, when we are actively participating in the eternal present moment. And the proof is in the pudding. Live more and more fully in the present moment, with your worries and manipulations quiet, and see how well you thrive!

## Spirit Acting in Everyday Lives

On close rational contemplation, neither lilies nor ravens sit around and do nothing all day. That certainly wasn't what Jesus was recommending. What ravens and lilies do is participate fully in the unfolding of each new moment. Ravens are acutely aware of what's happening around them – they're masters of the present moment. They respond instantly to opportunities that arise to find food and sustain their lives. Lilies likewise have their inherent God-given nature just as human beings do, and they naturally participate in their environment – the air, water, soil, and sunlight – to live their lives.

> The more I observe financially successful people who are also spiritually grounded and quite joyful in their lives, the more I see the same thing: These people succeed with smiles on their faces and joy in their hearts because they are living continually in the here and now.

They are heads-up all the time. They don't get lost in worries and dragged down in fear-based thoughts. Rather, they observe with all their senses what's happening around them; and with full cognitive and intuitive involvement in the present moment, they respond to opportunities and act spontaneously, with confidence and wisdom.

Where do they get this inner quality of confidence, wisdom, and right action? To answer this question, we're back where we started – and again, Jesus said it best: "Not my will, but thine, O Lord." These people have their creative minds open to tap their higher integrated intelligence, their hearts open to the inflow of God's love and communion with people around them, and their souls listening and responding to guidance from the Holy Spirit by whatever name.

They're winning because they're plugged in to a greater intelligence and wisdom than their ego intelligence and wisdom. They are heartful participants in God's creation, rather than fighting and worrying their way through life. They've found the effortless way to succeed. And so can we all.

Jesus rounded out that flow of words I've just quoted by

saying, "Provide yourselves with purses that do not grow old, with a treasure that does not fail, where no thief approaches and no moth destroys. For where your treasure is, there will your heart be also."

Again, we're back to the heart, which Jesus clearly considered primary. These words tell us without question that holding our mind's attention to our heart is primary in his view. If our hearts are caught in anxious struggling to survive, as we amass our treasures of physical and mental things, then our hearts are going to be polluted with negative emotions and strivings.

Over and over again in different words, we hear the basic suggestion that we open our hearts to love and be receptive to spiritual guidance, and then all things we need will come to us – that simple. Jesus says to trust life, trust God's creation to sustain us. As long as we hold our mind's attention here where wisdom and love can inflow into our hearts, there's nothing to worry about. God's creation shall flourish.

He concludes with this final reassurance about letting go of fear: "For this reason I say to you, don't be worried about your life, about what you will eat or what you will drink; or for your body, about what you will put on. Is not life more than food, and the body more than clothing?"

## Faith in God – Really

Even though many people try to be manipulative and trusting at the same time, ultimately, we do have to choose. The Bible tells us we can't "serve God and serve Mammon" at the same time. We can't stand with one foot grounded in an ego-based, fearful, manipulative attitude toward life and the other foot grounded in a love-based, trusting faith in God. Put psychologically, we can't focus our mind on our past-future worries and plots and at the same time focus on our present-moment participation in the unfolding of heaven on Earth. We must choose.

I used to think that having *faith in God* and *believing in God* were one and the same thing. Now I see that they're exact opposites. Believing in God means living at a conceptual mental level where you hold a hopeful attitude and positive assumption that God is there and will sustain you. This is a scary way to live because, by the nature of belief, you don't really know if it's true or not. Such a belief generates loads of fear and doubt – because what if it's not true?

> On the other hand, having faith in God is an actual spiritual experience based on a direct inner connection totally beyond beliefs, hopes, and concepts. Having faith in God is a secure feeling because of the genuine heart connection entirely beyond the scope of thoughts and beliefs.

When Jesus would lose patience with his followers (which he seems to have done quite often), he would say, "Oh ye of little faith!" His frustration must have emerged from clearly pointing toward the direct experience of spiritual sustenance and then realizing that the people he was teaching weren't really hearing what he was saying.

> His spiritual power to guide people into the kingdom of heaven on Earth was effective only for those people who had already awakened enough to where they were ready to hear what he was saying, and allow his love and wisdom to guide them into the eternal present moment.

In your own case, what do you think and feel about all this? Do you live your life based on beliefs you hope are true, or on faith and trust based on an inner experience of direct connection with your spiritual core of being?

# Reflection Time

*Let me offer you a gentle flow of words . . . and as you read the words, which are based fully on Jesus' words, see how your mind and heart respond.*

*First of all, just tune in to your breathing . . . the air flowing in and out of your nose . . . the movements in your chest and belly as you breathe . . . and the feelings in your heart right now . . . allow your thoughts to become quiet as you expand your awareness to include your whole body, here in this present moment . . . let go of your worries . . . and turn your mind's full attention to your heart . . . and to the presence of God's guidance in your heart . . . feel free to stop all your struggles, and instead trust in the higher wisdom and order of the world . . . open up and surrender to the subtle guidance of Spirit in your life . . . and tune directly in to the will and love of your Creator . . .*

# Pause & Experience

# 10

# "Be still, and know that I am God"

In a direct quote from God in Psalms 46, God gives, long before Jesus was born, what for me has always been the primary meditation commandment, and also the driving psychological dictum on how to manage our minds so as to connect directly with the divine. The commandment comes in two steps, and you'll find that I've therefore structured my meditation program in two steps.

The first step toward communing directly with God is another of those ultimate two-word statements: "Be still." In all of the world's most powerful meditation traditions, we must first of all quiet our nonstop mental chatter if we're to shift into a spiritual state of mind in which we're receptive to deep contact with Spirit.

> As long as the ego is chattering inside our minds, with all its busy comments, judgments, worries, plots, and plans, we simply cannot hear the voice of God. Jesus doesn't push into our consciousness. Spirit patiently waits for us to quiet our minds and tune in to our deeper awareness, before becoming active in our lives.

Psalms 37 sheds additional light on this mental-shifting process. Here, we're instructed to "Be still before the Lord, and wait patiently for him." Again, this statement expresses exactly the process of successful meditation. Not only are we to quiet our minds, we're also to remain calmly in this quiet-mind quality of consciousness – and wait for whatever will happen.

In the final, meditation section of this book I'm going to teach you the most effective way we've found to date for doing exactly what God seems to require of us psychologically in order for our mortal consciousness to come into synch with divine consciousness. I've already given you a taste of this process at the end of the previous chapter, where you explored your mind's ability to shift its focus away from the cognitive chatter in your head toward full involvement with your experience in the present moment.

> Because it's difficult to "think" and "experience" at the same time, if you want to still your mind, the most effective way to do this is to turn your attention toward two or more sensory happenings in the here and now.

## Be Still – By Being Here Now

As I've described in detail in *Quiet Your Mind*, I was involved in cognitive research early in my career for the National Institutes of Health in which we discovered that a person can focus on one sensory stimulation and also continue thinking. But as soon as you focus on two separate sensory happenings at the same time, your flow of thoughts stops.

This research indicates exactly how you can act in your mind to "be still" whenever you want to. Just develop a strong mental habit of turning your attention to one sensory event and then expand your awareness to include a second sensory event at the same time. And lo and behold, your mind has become still! I don't care what the perceptual inputs you focus on are – perhaps the singing of a bird, the sight of a sunset, a great three-part harmony in a country-western tune, the touch of your lover's fingertips, the soft sound of your lover's breathing. Whatever you choose, the trick is to expand your awareness to be aware of two or more sensations at the same time.

It does take a bit of practice to get good at this expansion of your attention. Let me again walk you through this "be still" process so that you begin to learn it by heart. This is the second step for entering into the "heart-path" meditation that Jesus encouraged – the first step being to *remember that you want to* move through this process.

Even as you read these words, also be aware of the air flowing in and out of your nose – the actual sensation you feel! Notice how tuning in to this ongoing sensation brings a special physical awareness to your nose and your head. And now allow your awareness to expand to include the movements in your chest and belly as you breathe. Feel your chest expanding when you inhale, and your stomach relaxing and bulging out a bit. And as you exhale, feel the muscles contract in your belly and your chest contract in size.

> As you stay aware of these two different sensations – the air flowing in and out of your nose, and the movements in your chest and belly as you breathe – you'll find that your thoughts will temporarily stop altogether while you maintain this sensory awareness.

If you remain fully aware of your breathing for a number of breaths and automatically quiet your thoughts in the process, you are "waiting patiently" . . . and yes, things will start happening. Almost always, you'll find that your awareness naturally expands to include also the feelings in your heart . . . and there you are, with your focus of attention exactly where Jesus suggests – on your heart experience. Then as you breathe, your awareness will naturally expand another major step to where you're aware of your whole body at once, here in this present moment.

This natural four-step expansion of consciousness is what meditation is all about, no matter which culture you drop into, because this is how God created us. It's simply how the mind works when we do what the Bible suggests. "Be still . . ."

## Listening . . .

As long as you're thinking all the time, lost in thought, you're in "broadcast mode," in which, instead of listening and receiving, you're talking and broadcasting. There's nothing wrong with thinking. We all love to think, and our thoughts can lead us to marvelous things. The problem that seems to have plagued people just as much two or three thousand years ago as it does now is that the talk-talk function of our minds seems to have mostly taken over, so that very seldom, if at all, are we quiet in our minds and open to receive inner guidance.

> One of the strange things about Christian practice in general is that we're taught to pray to God – meaning to talk to God – but we're seldom taught to be still and listen to God's voice within us.

Most people when they pray, talk nonstop. "Dear God, please help me, I need . . . blah blah blah . . ." for the entire prayer, then the praying time is over – and never for even ten seconds has the person shifted into receive mode, with thoughts quiet, the mind still, and Spirit therefore able to speak to this person's heart and soul.

What's your own experience in this regard? Do you pray? And

if you do, how much of the time is your mind still and your soul receptive to listening to God? Take a little time here if you want, to put the book aside and reflect on your mental habits. Is your mind quiet now and then? Do the words "Be still" mean anything to you? And are you interested in learning how to quiet your mind?

# Pause & Reflect

*Tune in to the air flowing in and out of your nose . . . the movements in your chest and belly as you breathe . . . the feelings in your heart right now . . . your whole body, here in this present moment . . . and now open yourself to experience stillness in your mind . . . and be open to a new experience . . .*

# Pause & Experience

## The Intuitive Flash – Spirit Acting!

When you quiet your mind and patiently experience the present moment unfolding in your life, you'll often find that sudden flashes of intuitive insight come to you. Sometimes this happens in a very subtle way, but sometimes in a sudden flash as the whole idea or solution comes to you. At other times, you might experience a subtle inner intuitive voice speaking to you, giving you insight and guidance in your life.

This quiet state of mind is definitely where higher guidance inflows. I don't care if you label these as intuitive flashes, as Spirit acting in your life, or whatever. What's important is regularly pausing to quiet your mind and open to this deeper level of wisdom, knowing, and realization.

Most of us have deeply ingrained think-think habits that dominate our awareness. It's not, at first, all that easy to quiet that nonstop stream of thoughts that rush through your mind almost every waking moment. I'm teaching you the most effective method for quieting that stream of thoughts whenever you want to. If you find that you want or need further guidance in this quiet-mind process, please feel free to go online (www.johnselby.com) and explore the specific psychological and meditation programs you'll find for developing, step by step, the inner capacity to manage your mind to your advantage.

Throughout, what's important to hold in mind is that you have the power to take charge of your mind, quiet your thoughts, and, in essence, obey the commandment that God has given to us – the specific instruction on how to access divine guidance and love in our lives. "Be still . . ."

## "Know" That I Am God

When I was at seminary, I kept bringing this primary biblical quote, "Be still, and know that I am God," to the attention of my professors – they were mostly wonderful, brilliant seekers of truth – and asking them what the Hebrew term for "know" (as used in the Bible) actually meant. Are we supposed to be still, and think about God? Is knowing a thought process as we're usually taught?

> Is God telling us to "be still," and at the same time delve into deep theological reflection on what it means to be God? Or are we supposed to truly be still and know directly, beyond all words and beliefs, the direct experiential reality of God? How do we "know that I am God"?

The Old Testament professor at my seminary, Professor Muellenberg, was close to the end of his life when I studied under him; in fact, he died while I was at seminary. This man touched my heart deeply, and also provided the best answer to my question about "knowing." He clarified that the same Hebrew word was used in the statement "Be still, and *know* that I am God" as was used in Genesis in the statement "Adam *knew* Eve, his wife, and she conceived and bore Cain. Cain *knew* his wife, and she conceived and bore Enoch. And Adam *knew* his wife again, and she bore a son," and so forth.

> In other words, God is inviting us to "know" him at the same level of intimacy that we experience in our deepest relating – heart to heart. We're being invited to experience God as directly as possible, in a way that, at some spiritual level, could include the creation of a new being, the union of human and divine, and whatever consequences come from that union.

I was quite honestly shocked by what this professor shared with me. At first, I thought he was pulling my leg in a joke, but when I met his eyes I saw that he was absolutely serious. At the same time, there was a sparkle in his eyes that showed me that all of this was beyond even his brilliant intellect, touching truths that the thinking mind simply cannot fathom.

As I came to realize that God had commanded us to quiet our minds and commune with Spirit at the most intimate heart-to-heart level, my whole life changed at seminary. This was when I became insistent that we develop a meditative dimension to our training to become ministers in the Presbyterian Church – which led to increased excitement and adventure, and also to my final separation from the traditional church.

> Once I realized that Christianity was vastly more than *thoughts about* God, that it was instead an opportunity to *know* God directly – I realized that that was the expe-

rience I wanted. Ultimately yes, I had to leave the church to get it, but I've never regretted my choice to go for direct "knowing" rather than staying stuck in talk-about beliefs.

## I Am God . . .

There's yet another dimension to "Be still, and know that I am God." If I sidestepped this final issue, I wouldn't be fully honest with you, so here goes – even though traditional Christian theologians burned many a humble soul for stating the same thing. You're going to discover this for yourself anyway, if you haven't already, when you begin quieting your mind and opening up to communion directly with God. So let me state it clearly here.

Almost always in meditation when people of any faith follow the heart path, quiet their minds, and open up to their unique experience of oneness with God, they find that, at a certain point, something happens that forever changes their sense of who they are and what life is all about.

They experience their personal mortal sense of identity temporarily merging with the infinite eternal Identity . . . until all of a sudden there's absolutely no sense of separation between them and . . . God.

Christianity as a theology has been built upon the belief that human beings are fallen angels – that we're born separate from God. In direct contrast, in Hindu, Buddhist, and Taoist teachings, there is no question that, at our core of being, we possess the spark of God ourselves. And in meditation, we begin to experience this directly, to "know that I am God." In deep meditation, there exists in our hearts no sense of spiritual separation between God and us. We are God in individualized mortal form – and as we wake up and realize our divine nature, this truth becomes experientially obvious.

Ultimately, the duality between God and God's creation is a theological concept that doesn't stand up in the reality of meditation. Likewise in this Judeo-Christian commandment to "Know that I am God," we are challenged, in my understanding and experience, to be still so we can know who we really are: a spark of individualized divine consciousness directly in communion with our Creator.

We now know that there were many less politically successful early Christian sects, such as the Gnostics, who taught, believed, and experienced the divinity of human consciousness.

But the Catholic Church grew steadily in dominance and mercilessly fought against and destroyed these more mystical groups, to the point that, a few hundred years after Jesus' death, almost all mention of mystical union in Christian meditation had been wiped out of the four remaining Gospels, and all formal church practice.

As Shakespeare would say, "What a falling off was there . . ." This book is here to raise the issue again of what we naturally discover when we quiet our minds, and look to see the truth. I'm here to challenge you gently, if you want the challenge, to explore what happens in your mind, in your heart, in your core spiritual experience when you learn to quiet your noisy thoughts, to be still and patient in your mind – so you can discover for yourself the truth of the matter.

## Eliciting the Experience

How can you best move in this direction if you want to turn your mind's attention in a particular direction to discover what truths await you there?

The most effective psychological technique, as I teach in many of my books and online courses, is to say to yourself particular focus phrases specially designed to aim your mind's power of attention where you indicate by the words.

The final meditation section of this book is based on the psychological fact that by saying to yourself specific statements, you do shift your consciousness in that direction, and thus awaken your potential for new experience. To end this chapter on a pragmatic note, I'd like to suggest that you explore what happens when you not only read "Be still, and know that I am God," but also say this to yourself a number of times, as a focus phrase of the highest order.

#  Reflection Time

*Let me guide you through this process, and when you learn the process by heart you'll be able to move through this on your own. You can also go to the website (www.johnselby.com) and let my voice in streamed audio guide you through the experience until you make it your own:*

*Go ahead and get relaxed – give yourself permission to enjoy the next few minutes . . . begin to be aware of your breathing . . . the air flowing in and out of your nose . . . the movements in your chest and belly as you breathe . . . and the feelings in your heart . . . allow your thoughts to become quiet as you expand your awareness to include your whole body, here in this present moment . . . you can let go of your worries . . . turn your mind's full attention to the inflow of love in your heart.*

*When you're ready, you can say the following words to yourself, allowing a breath or two for each part of the statement. Exhale as you say the words to yourself . . . and as you inhale, experience whatever the words stimulate within your awareness:*

*"Be still . . . (breathe . . .)*

*and know . . . (breathe . . .)*

*that I am God . . ." (breathe . . .)*

# Pause & Experience

# 11

# "Love your neighbor as you love yourself"

Love is the central teaching of Jesus. And again, Jesus the psychologist gives us a reality-based commandment that is within our ability to attain. Knowing that we cannot love another person *more than* we love ourselves, he challenges us to love those around us just *as much* as we love ourselves. Furthermore he puts the focus on loving ourselves, so that we can, in turn, love others.

Traditional Christianity and especially certain born-again sects have tended to judge negatively any efforts we might make to improve our relationship with ourselves. In this mode, the whole New Age movement was put down for being self-centered.

But the truth is, as long as our hearts are closed to our own selves, we simply can't open our hearts to another person. So the commandment "Love your neighbor as you love your-self" indicates clearly that we should first of all focus atten-tion on learning to accept and love ourselves unconditionally, so that we can then love those around us in like manner.

According to the Protestant Church of my childhood, we were supposed always to be loving, sweet, and kind to everyone around us. But I remember that this Christian effort to be especially lov-ing usually came across as forced and even phony, because no matter how hard sincere Christians tried to be loving to others, as long as they felt unloving toward themselves, the whole thing was hopeless.

Jesus instead points out that we must first learn to accept our-selves just as we are, if we're ever to love our neighbor whole-heartedly. And he certainly never suggested that we should try the impossible and love our neighbors more than we love our-selves. Love just doesn't work that way.

Especially when we've been programmed to believe that we're hopeless sinners, it's almost impossible to love our-selves just as we are. This is why we must choose between the theology path and the heart path in reading the Bible – because we keep running up against these polar-opposite visions of who we are and what life is all about.

If we believe that we're hopeless sinners at the core of our being, then we can't love ourselves, so we're not going to be able to love one another. Seen in that light, it's not hard to choose which to throw out and which to live with. And then we need to dig in and learn how to let go of the various negative concepts we hold that keep us from loving ourselves just as we are.

## What about You?

I know from experience with a great many students that letting go of self-judgment, and loving yourself just as you are, can be a lot easier said than done. From an early age, most of us were strongly influenced by parents, teachers, siblings, and all the rest who quite definitely didn't accept us just as we were. And why didn't they? Because, of course, they didn't accept themselves just as they were. This negative self-judgment just keeps getting passed down generation after generation, reinforced by religious beliefs that teach us to perceive even toddlers as sinful beings.

What is it about your own self that you don't accept, or that you judge as bad, inadequate, somehow ugly, or downright sinful? Even though Jesus said, "Don't judge," all societies possess a long list of things that are bad and sinful. We're teethed on a code of ethics, on a set of values we're supposed to live our lives by. And why do we have this set of values, this list of rules that we try to stuff our lives into? Because from birth, we grew up with people who didn't trust or love their own nature, and therefore didn't trust ours either.

We're looking right at one of the most terrible aspects of human culture, which we're hopefully learning to transcend. A child forms its sense of goodness or sinfulness very early in its life, based not on its own experience but on how others judge it. And this primal negative judgment that we all received lies at the core of our opinion of ourselves, and of everyone around us.

Traditional Christianity does not see human nature as good – in fact, the whole Christ-our-Savior routine doesn't work if we already see ourselves as good. Only if we can be conditioned to see ourselves as hopelessly bad are we susceptible to priestly pressure to accept Jesus as our savior, rather than as our spiritual mentor and guide.

So when I suggest, as did Jesus, that you accept yourself as okay just as you are, so that you can also love your neighbor wholeheartedly, you're naturally liable to run up against deep ingrained attitudes that say no, you're not okay just as you are. What can you do about this early childhood programming?

There's only one thing you can do – chuck that programming! I've known people who spent year after year in therapy trying to work, step by step, through all their ingrained negative attitudes so as to be finally free of them – but to no avail.

> Ultimately, you can't struggle to escape your sinful nature; all you can do is choose to stop seeing yourself that way. It's a choice. At some point, perhaps right now, you simply decide that you're going to accept yourself, and open your heart to yourself, just as you are. And you do it!

Easier said than done? No – *easy* to do, with the right mental tool. And here's the tool you'll need for accomplishing this leap of faith, a tool that if you use it regularly, will serve you magnificently. All you need do to move yourself in the direction of loving yourself just as you are is to state your intent, by saying to yourself the words: "I love myself, just as I am."

These particular words carry the power to resonate deeper and deeper into your psyche every time you say them. Yes, this is a definite act of purposeful reprogramming – and it's absolutely required, if you're to override the negative programming you received early on.

The question is this: After you say the words, and remain aware of your breaths coming and going, and the feelings in your heart, does anything happen? Do you feel a slight softening in your heart? Just experiment (at first maybe just for a few breaths) and see for yourself how it feels to love yourself just as you are.

Even early in your training with the new meditation you're learning in this book, the words I suggest you say to yourself on a regular basis will surely elicit a slight positive response. Notice: Do you like that response, so that you want to move in that direction more and more? If so, you're already on your way to success in your heart.

# ☘ Pause & Reflect

*Take some free moments now and try this for real. After reading this paragraph, put the book aside . . . tune in to your breathing . . . the feelings in your heart . . . and say to yourself a few times, "I love myself, just as I am." And be open to a new experience!*

# ☘ Pause & Experience

## All the Help We Can Get

In the past, when working with people in traditional therapy, I would offer them this psychological tool to work with regularly, along with a guided audio CD that they could listen to at home to guide them through this emotional healing process. If the client wasn't spiritually inclined, I'd be somewhat limited in the guidance I could offer, because I wouldn't want to push my spiritual inclinations onto the client. But in the context of this overtly spiritual book, I can readily say to you that there's another great help you can turn to in this process of learning to love yourself more.

In your meditations on learning to love and accept yourself just as you are, you can openly ask for help from God, from Spirit, from Jesus, from Magdalena . . .

We do need all the help we can get when it comes to transcending ingrained attitudes and emotions. And that help is always available to us – if only we open up and ask for it. Hold in mind that, as mentioned before, a primary quality of Spirit is that this spiritual force doesn't ever push into our lives uninvited. There's an infinite source of healing love in the universe available to each of us each new moment of our lives. But we must choose to ask for it to inflow into our hearts and lives – or it simply won't.

> How do you manage to ask for God's love to come into your heart? You know me well enough by now to guess the answer: You simply go ahead and say it – "I open my heart to the inflow of God's love." Or perhaps you might say to yourself, "My heart is open to God's healing love."

As you breathe into their impact, these words will resonate throughout your being, more and more each time you say them. After a couple of weeks of practicing such a heart-healing meditation, when you say the words, you will immediately go very deeply into this experience. You will feel love flowing into your heart, filling your being and, in the process, giving you all the power you need in order to love yourself unconditionally. It's that simple – ask for it, and you get it. But if you don't act and say the words, chances are it won't happen.

## The Nature of Love

The Bible states clearly the primal three-word declaration that "God is love." That's an intense equation that I often like to bring to the fore, because it shows just how ultimate the word, the feeling, and the experience of love are, from a spiritual perspective.

Love indeed is the creative force of the universe – with all that implies. Love is what makes the world go 'round. Love is what Christianity is supposed to be all about. Love is the essence of Jesus' teachings. Love is what heals all wounds. Love is the main gift we have to give each other. Love is the connective tissue of the spiritual body. Love is all there is . . .

> When we don't love ourselves, we deny ourselves the vital essence that keeps our spiritual body alive and well. We need love on a daily, even a moment-to-moment basis, if

we're to feel good and powerful, and plugged into divine inspiration.

When we judge ourselves as unlovable, when we close our hearts to our own selves, we starve ourselves. What's worse, we deny Spirit; we shut Spirit out of our lives. And when we do this, not only do we suffer, but our neighbor suffers as well. Because when we don't love ourselves, we can't love those around us. The whole thing breaks down. We can neither give nor receive love, if we don't first regularly open our hearts to the inflow of love into our own core of being.

All we need to do, for love to flourish in our lives, is open our hearts and let the love flow in. And all we need to do, for that love to flow in, is say to ourselves regularly – and mean it! – "I love myself, just as I am . . . and I open my heart to let God's love flow in!"

Stop judging yourself. Toss out all beliefs, attitudes, and negative one-liners that close your heart. Focus on the infinite love that God gives us entirely for free – to share. There's not much more to say here – except – do it!

#  Reflection Time

*After reading this paragraph, feel free to put the book aside . . . tune in to your breathing . . . your heart . . . then say to yourself, "I give myself permission to feel good," and just relax into the brightness of this present moment . . .*

*When you're ready, turn your attention to your heart again . . . breathe into whatever feelings or lack of them you find there . . . and say to yourself, "I accept and love myself, just as I am." Stay aware of your feelings and breathing as those words reverberate throughout your being. Don't expect anything earth-shaking, just move a tiny step in the direction of loving yourself unconditionally.*

*And if you want to, you can also say, "I open my heart to receive God's love . . ." and allow those words to encourage love to come flowing in . . . and as always, be open to a new experience . . .*

# Pause & Experience

# 12

# "Love one another as I have loved you"

I hope you're beginning to see how all of these Jesus quotes are intimately related and, when taken together, offer a unified vision of Jesus' meditative approach to emotional healing and spiritual awakening. Certainly, the quote we worked with in the last chapter, "Love your neighbor as you love yourself," isn't complete until we bring in this final "love" commandment: "Love one another as I have loved you."

How did Jesus love? I remember spending a whole year at seminary possessed with the question of how Jesus actually did love the people he related with. Have you ever thought about this question? If we're to love each other the same way Jesus loved his friends and followers – and, indeed, his enemies – we need to develop some sort of understanding of the nature, quality, and expression of Jesus' love for those around him.

This chapter is going to lead us into some explosive realizations in answering this question, based on the evidence actually found in the Gospels. So hang in there as we jump onto this roller coaster of love.

First of all, what did Jesus actually say about love? Let me share with you a few quotes that are of great help, beginning with his vastly important declaration evoked when a scribe came up and asked him, "Which commandment is the first of all?"

Jesus answered, "The first is, 'The Lord our God is one; and you shall love the Lord your God with all your heart, and with all your soul, and with all your mind, and with all your strength.' The second is this, 'You shall love your neighbor as you love yourself.' There is no other commandment greater than these."

Talk about an amazing sentence! First of all, he clarifies that God is one infinite whole – there aren't diverse gods of this and that – and furthermore that our relationship with this infinite Creator and Sustainer is a loving relationship of the utmost depth and breadth, leaving nothing out. All our primary individual qualities of heart, soul, mind, and strength are to be held focused on our loving relationship with God. That's the first commandment: to love God totally all the time.

The second commandment, which he calls greater than all the other laws and commandments that the Hebrews (and later the Christians) revered, in effect, turns our attention directly toward how we love ourselves and, in turn, how we love those around us: "You shall love your neighbor as you love yourself."

Then elsewhere Jesus expands dramatically on this initial statement: "A new commandment I give to you," he told his followers, "that you love one another, even as I have loved you."

## How Did Jesus Love?

Jesus went one step further in expressing the nature of his own love. He said to his disciples: "As the Father has loved me, so have

I loved you." His love carried the power, the glory, the infinite unconditional love of God. And this is how we're supposed to love one another? Wow. That seems like an impossible challenge: to love one another as Jesus loved, which is in the same mode as God loved him.

By the way, as mentioned earlier, I don't necessarily see God as a father figure, as the words of the commandment might imply. Jesus' relationship with God was stated in the traditional masculine format because the entire mental construct of the Aramaic language he spoke perceived God as masculine. We don't need to get hung up on the "God the Father" issue. But Jesus' powerful suggestion that we love one another as he loved us, which is how God also loves him, this is something to dwell on deeply and often, a realization to open up to and embrace.

Within the context of this unconditional love, Jesus also suggests that people "love your enemies, and do good and lend, expecting nothing in return. Be merciful, even as your Father is merciful." Again, we're being challenged to act in the world with the same love and power through which God acts.

**Jesus goes on with his remarkable statement: "Judge not, and you will not be judged; condemn not, and you will not be condemned; forgive, and you will be forgiven; give, and it will be given to you."**

In another gospel, there are similar words: "I say to you that hear, do good to those who hate you, bless those who curse you, pray for those who abuse you. To him who strikes you on the cheek, offer the other also; and from him who takes away your coat do not withhold even your shirt. And as you wish that men would do to you, do so to them."

This is the kind of love that Jesus is talking about, the kind in which we remain in love regardless of the situation. Even when Jesus was being crucified on the cross, he stayed in love, forgiving those who were killing him. And in this process of remaining in a state of unconditional love, he seems to have approached and moved through even his own death in a state of acceptance, grace, and spiritual bliss.

Whether or not he later physically rose from the dead (this superhuman act is portrayed in very few chapters of the Gospels, and witnessed by very few people), what comes shining through is his example – his truly superhuman capacity even in extremis to live in love, and to radiate God's love outward to all those around him.

This is his challenge to us: that we love with the same depth and power that he and God love . . . this is how great our own capacity for loving seems to be.

## Jesus Loving His Mother

Curiously, Jesus doesn't tell us to love one another in the way that most people tend to: trying to protect other people from emotional upset.

> So often we think that, to be loving, we should try never to hurt other people's feelings. But Jesus in no way loved protectively, as most of us do. In fact, on close inspection, Jesus didn't seem to assume responsibility for other people's emotions at all.

Consider this. We're supposed to love and honor our parents, right? That's one of the many values taken from Hebrew law that we carry forth into our present "family values" code of ethics. But from what we can glean from the Gospels, Jesus lived his life without worrying at all about other people's feelings.

Especially with his mother, he did things that just broke her heart – but he didn't change his choices in life even though those choices upset Mary so terribly. Imagine the Passion Play from his mother's point of view. I mean, Jesus didn't have to ride into Jerusalem asking for trouble with the authorities. He knew they were out to get him, and yet into Jerusalem he rode – knowing full well that he could get killed in the process. How could a nice

Jewish boy do such a heartless thing to his mother as to court violent public death with her watching?

But he did it. And this shows us something remarkably important about how Jesus walked the heart path. Each step of the way, he made his decisions not based on the consequences of his actions and the impact on those who loved him.

> According to his own commandment, he had fully surrendered his heart and mind and soul to God, and thus allowed Spirit to guide him in the unfolding of each new moment. As long as he acted in Spirit, he was acting in love – even when his actions made his mother go through the must excruciating trauma. That's the intensity and devotion of love he's challenging us to experience as well.

That's how we're supposed to love our neighbor. Not by trying to protect his or her feelings from being hurt, as we often do in a romantic or family involvement. Instead, every moment in a relationship we're challenged to open up our hearts to the loving guidance of our core spiritual voice, and then act in the spirit of love, whatever we do.

Jesus loved everyone around him without judgment, without fear, without restrictions. He allowed God's love to flow through him, into the hearts of others. And he still does. Shall we, as well?

Pause if you want, and look to your heart right now. How is this discussion impacting your feelings, and your thoughts? What would happen in your life if you spontaneously allowed your spiritual voice to guide your actions, regardless of how those actions might affect the feelings and lives of those around you?

## Jesus for All

Historically, we don't know anything specific about Jesus' sexual life. I think this works to our advantage because, in our intimate present-moment meditations, we're free to relate with Jesus as a spiritual presence from whatever our own sexual preference might be.

> If you're gay, this means Jesus can come to you in your own natural sexual disposition. Why not? Spirit comes to us in the mode that is most us. That's why it's so important to also include Maria Magdalena in this whole picture, so that if and when we want to tune in to a female spiritual link to God, perhaps even a gay female spiritual link, then we can do just that.

As a practicing heterosexual, I've already shared with you what works best for me – that Jesus and Maria Magdalena were a couple, perhaps married, perhaps not. After all, she, not one of his male friends, was the one who sensuously massaged his feet with oil. She was there at his side consistently – she's his female counterpart.

This works for me, but please feel free to open up and approach your divine link with whatever works for you. Spirit is beyond physical sexuality, to be sure, but will meet us at our own living core of being, which, while we're alive in human bodies, includes our sexual presence and preference.

## Resurrection – A Female Account

Christianity as a theological religion is centered entirely upon the historic "fact" that Jesus was killed, was in the grave three days, and then, like Lazarus, was mysteriously raised up from the dead into new life – in his physical body. As the very brief gospel account relates, 40 days afterward, this physical body was then lifted up into the heavens.

Curiously, even though the validity of these resurrection events is front and center to the entire Christian theological belief system, none of Jesus' male disciples witnessed the Easter Sunday encounter.

Only two women, the two who were closest to Jesus and therefore in total emotional meltdown at the time, actually reported seeing Jesus alive in his physical body right after his crucifixion, in the garden that Sunday morning. In fact, the entire born-again resurrection dimension upon which Christianity is built is based almost entirely on that all-female account.

Let me share with you something that happened in my own family that somehow relates to this ancient account of death and life after death. Three days after my father died, my mother was alone in her bedroom, when suddenly she opened her eyes and saw my father standing there beside her bed, very much in his physical body. He talked to her, she heard his physical voice, she said she could even smell slightly his distinctive olfactory presence.

Mom told me later that she was certain he was definitely there before her physically – and not only that, Jesus was standing beside him, holding his hand. She saw Jesus there in his physical body as well. My father spoke and told my mother that everything was okay, that he would be waiting for her and that she was to be joyful, not sad. Then, just as quickly as he'd come, Dad disappeared, and Jesus with him.

I relate this account because it's as close as I've personally come to an event similar to what Maria Magdalena and Jesus' mother Mary experienced that first Easter morning, when in the depths of utter despair, they suddenly encountered Jesus and an angel of God standing before them. Who can say at what level such experiences are real? My mother felt without question that her experience was physically real. Apparently the two Marys felt the same.

Jesus' male disciples readily accepted the two women's mysterious account, partly because Jesus' physical body had gone missing (there are multiple explanations for this) and partly because the disciples had assumed that Jesus wouldn't just be killed and buried and that would be that. The account of Jesus appearing physically to the two women was vastly easier to accept and live with than the account that Jesus was dead and gone forever.

We will never know what happened two thousand years ago as a historical event. Rationally, this is therefore a moot point. We can believe whatever we want to believe, but historically we won't get beyond the belief level.

So what can we do? Live our spiritual lives based on hopeful but unverifiable beliefs of physical resurrection, or shift from thoughts, ideas, and imaginings – toward our own inner experience of Jesus directly coming to us as Spirit in the present moment, and deeply touching our lives? That's the choice – past history, or present experience.

## God Is Love

When we choose to let go of the past, imaginings, and all the rest, and tune in to our direct link with the love of God in our present lives, we come to the point where we experience the love that transcends mortal bounds, that is infinite, and that welcomes us into this infinite communion with the divine. Earlier, we delved deeply into the ancient meditative commandment "Be still, and know that I am God." I'd like to enhance that challenge with one of my favorite quotes from the gospel according to John:

> "He who does not love, does not know God; for God is love." This statement certainly clarifies the heart path, where we ourselves must love in order to know God. This conscious act of choosing to love is the direct path to the divine.

Unfortunately, a great many people live their lives with very little love flowing through their hearts. We've seen why – because love is not present when fear or judgment dominates our hearts and minds. When anxiety grips us, love falls away. And when this happens, not only do we feel the pain of fear gripping us, we also feel the agony of being separated from God. God is love – no love, no experience of God.

It's the same with judgment. Jesus said, just don't do it. But when we do, we suffer that primordial expulsion from the Garden. We become cut off from God and from God's love. We might struggle heroically (and a bit desperately) to find God through thinking magnificent flights of religious thought. But thoughts won't get us there.

Therefore we have been given the primary commandment from the Old Testament: "Be still, and know that I am God." And in this stillness, lo and behold, we find that love does come flowing in. Stop the thoughts, receive the love. That's what we're going to focus more and more intently on encouraging: the actual act of participating in the love of God.

## Compassion in Motion

Love makes us feel wonderful. Love brings us alive in the present moment. Love is the bond that holds hearts together. So, of course, we'd all like to get a whole lot of love amassed in our possession, and hold on to it so that we're rich in love.

But as you'll agree from your own inner experience, love is not something we can store up in our hearts. One of the primary qualities of love is that it exists only in action, in sharing, in movement; it's a free-flowing power that can fill our hearts, but we can't then screw a cap on the heart when it's full of love and thus possess a secure quantity of love for future use.

> Love comes and goes freely – and comes again. Jesus said that the more we give, the more we receive – this is the nature of God's love. As love flows outward, it flows in.

This is my experience in my relationship with Jesus and Spirit in the oneness of God's presence. All I need to do to bring the flow of love into my life is to choose to say sincerely, "My heart is open to receive God's love," and the love comes flowing in. And my natural response to this inflow of love is to share it with those around me. Otherwise the love begins to dry up.

I hope that this understanding of God's love as something we can't possess even for a moment becomes central in your approach to walking the heart path. Experiencing the inflow of love will always be new, just as all experience in the present moment is always new. And only when we stop our thoughts and become empty of the past, can we fill up with the present. That's just the fact of life, that's how God set this whole thing up, as far as I can see. That's how Jesus loved – and that's how we love. Spontaneous compassion in perpetual motion.

# ✿ Reflection Time

*Again, we've covered a lot of ground fast. It's time to pause, let the dust settle, and encourage you to put this book aside, so you can tune in to whatever's happening right now in your own heart and soul. I encourage you to drop out of reading for at least a few minutes now, so that you can let go of thoughts, and bring your mind's attention fully to the present moment. Discover what feelings, insights, even revelations might await you in the midst of your next few breaths . . .*

*Here in this present moment, turn your attention to feel:*

- *The air flowing in and out of your nose . . .*

- *The movements in your chest and belly as you breathe . . .*

- *The feelings in your heart right now . . .*

*Jesus said, "Love one another, as I have loved you." As you stay tuned in to a deep awareness of your breathing and your heart right now, go ahead and say to yourself, "My heart is open to receive God's healing love." Allow these words to reverberate throughout your heart, mind, and soul as you open to the loving presence of Jesus and Spirit in your life . . . and experience the love . . . flowing in . . .*

# ✿ Pause & Experience

# 13

# "Know the truth, and the truth will set you free"

As mentioned earlier, Jesus didn't command that we *think about* the truth, nor *reflect on* the truth, nor *believe in* the truth, nor *imagine* the truth. He didn't tell us to accept what others told us about the truth or even to follow what the Bible says about the truth. Instead, he told us quite bluntly to "*know* the truth" directly.

We talked earlier about the ancient meaning of this verb "to know" and how it refers to the ultimate intimate experience of being one with the truth. To know the truth is an act. It is an immersion. It is a surrender and a discovery and, most of all, it is an experience.

We know something is true when we experience it for ourselves. Everything else is an assumption, a belief, a projection, or just plain wishful thinking. But when we have an experience that feels valid to us at our core of being, then we know something to be true. I would go further and say that this knowing is something experienced in the heart. To know in your heart that something is true, is truly to know it.

So how do we realistically approach knowing the truth? What is the truth, after all? In some esoteric Gnostic Christian traditions of the early church, the truth was written with a big T and became Truth. This was very much in the spirit of the ancient Greek way of seeing the world, where there were absolute realities or Truths. In our age, we don't tend to perceive the world in absolute terms, and I don't often approach the truth as a timeless unchanging Truth. Instead, I find it more worthwhile to approach the truth as a feeling of realization and certainty, of knowing something at the depths of my being.

I also find it best to approach the truth as an experience that is always just emerging in the newness of each moment. We know the truth right now – and must let go of that experience of the truth in order to embrace the next moment's experience of truth. Does this make sense to you? For me, this is a vital differentiation.

> The truth seems ultimately to be nothing more – and nothing less – than the reality of the present moment, whatever that is for us right now. The truth is what is real. And if we have beliefs that aren't entirely congruent with reality, then these beliefs will constantly keep us from knowing the truth.

The truth is ever self-generating and thus infinite, and not to be confined in any of our limiting concepts of reality. The truth is also always changing, in that change is the only constant we find in the universe.

And how do we experience this truth? How do we know it directly? This experience seems to be an awareness and a feeling, a whole-body realization – this is the immediate interface that God gave us for knowing intimately the reality in which we live. Jesus is pointing us (as he so often does) toward the direct, total encounter, not just toward lofty notions of the mind. Yes, often thoughts do come to mind related to our experience of the truth, inspired thoughts that emerge from our whole-brain intuitive function, which does include deductive mentation. But these inspired thoughts transcend our usual level of thinking.

We sense reality and all the deeper spiritual dimensions of life not just through our five external sensory systems (seeing, hearing, tasting, touching, smelling) and resulting thoughts, but also through what, for lack of a better word, is called our *sixth* sense – that most direct feeling of encounter with the divine, with truth, with reality . . . with God.

I remember in one of Carlos Castaneda's remarkable books about the ancient Yaqui Indian teachings of Don Juan Mateus, that when Carlos asked his teacher what is real, Don Juan smiled, touched Carlos's chest, and said, "Reality is a feeling, right there." And indeed, in this light, the truth does seem to be a feeling, an intimate experience, which we know in our hearts and our whole-body sensory presence.

## Knowing the Truth – The Practice

Every time we tune in to our hearts and whole-body presence with our minds quiet and our souls receptive, we are in position to know the truth. It is to be hoped that this inner flash of encounter with reality happens often each day. I'm encouraging you to develop a regular meditation wherein you consciously tune in to the truth.

The "know the truth" practice, as we've been exploring all along, is basic: Turn your attention toward your breathing – that's truth right there! Experience the truth of your relationship with oxygen, the truth that, without oxygen on a moment-to-moment basis, you actually cease to exist as a physical presence on this planet.

Experience that truth even more deeply by exhaling and holding your breath a few moments, until you feel the pressure to inhale. That's the reality of your biological life – dig it! And equally, as you expand your awareness, feel your heart beating in your chest. The more you learn to feel this experiential level of reality, the deeper you move into the truth. The reality is that your heart and your breathing sustain your life. To feel that truth, rather than just think about it, is to enter into a higher level of consciousness.

When you look to your heart, you will never find the same experience there twice, as we've seen. So what will you find? That's the adventure – that's the pure pleasure and sometimes the extreme excitement of meditating on reality itself.

> It's always new, and sometimes it violates your concept of reality, so that you have to choose to deny the experience of the truth, or expand and adapt your concept of reality to embrace the truth.

Each time, how you manage your encounter with the truth is up to you – and no judgment, please. As with all of Jesus' commandments, this one seems to be given in the spirit of a challenge, of a direction to aim toward and move in as your daily spiritual practice.

## The Truth *Will* Set You Free

Is there really freedom in this life of ours? We have Freedom as a concept, a goal, and almost a religious and even political idol. But can we have the actual experience of being free? Jesus is saying most definitely yes. And here's how to attain true freedom: Know the truth.

> Freedom comes as we surrender to reality. It's that simple,

and spiritual teachers have known this forever. Now is the time for us to know it too – and know it in our hearts as an experience.

Through quieting the mind and opening up to the wisdom and insight Spirit brings us, we can know the truth directly and be set free. This true freedom is the aim of all meditation, as we simply look inward and experience the truth of what we find. Jesus knew this truth, and commanded his followers to know it too. So why do we mostly not do this?

Freedom is a scary thing. Do we really want to be free, or do we want to live our lives within set boundaries, regulations, and beliefs that limit what might happen in our lives? Security is seen as the opposite of freedom in many cases, and we do want to be secure because then we feel safe and sound and taken care of. And that's perfectly alright as far as I'm concerned. As Alan Watts said, we live in a two-hundred-percent reality where we can feel completely secure and feel completely free at the same time – if only we surrender to reality, to the truth.

This is what I've learned by meditating on the truth, on reality: that when my mind resists reality, refuses to accept the truth of the matter, I suffer and am insecure. There's nothing more dangerous than refusing to accept what's true, what's real – because when we fight reality, we get hurt.

But if we know the truth, if we accept reality and surrender to the totality of what is happening right now in our lives, something truly remarkable happens. We come into harmony with reality, we begin participating spontaneously in this reality; every cell resonates in congruence with every other cell so that the dance of life becomes confident, secure, and a pleasure.

For me, that's freedom – the freedom to participate fully in reality itself. When we are free of our attitudes and beliefs, our assumptions and projections, when we know the truth in our hearts, then an entirely new quality of living comes into us.

Spirit moves through us as we surrender to our deeper spiritual nature, which is to participate in the dance God is tapping out in our moment-to-moment heartbeat rhythm of life. Do you want this freedom to really be yourself?

Jesus pointed the way to this freedom. Look inward regularly, without judgment, without thoughts, without expectations – and experience what is real in your heart. That's what spirituality is all about, and it's so simple and easy, and yet for most of us so difficult and complex.

I hope that this book and its meditations offer a path that makes knowing the truth easy for you. Knowing the truth is a moment-to-moment affair. Our challenge is to tune in to the truth continually, so that we are continually being reborn into the freedom of the eternal present moment.

# ✌ Reflection Time

*Right now is when you know the truth – not sometime in the future or in the past. Whatever you're doing, this is the moment of truth.*

*You are reading these words, you are breathing, you have feelings in your heart, you are aware of your whole body at once. You are engaged in intimate interaction with your environment through all your senses and through your spiritual sense of communion as well . . . here you are, this is the truth you know. And this experiential truth is setting you continually free from your own past-tense programming.*

*Tune in to the air flowing in and out of your nose or mouth right now . . . feel the sensations being created by this flow . . . the reality of this sensation, the truth of your oneness with the air around you . . . experience it directly – know it!*

*Expand your awareness of the truth to include the movements in your chest and belly as you breathe . . . your continual expansion and contraction . . . the life force that stimulates your next breath in your solar plexus . . . feel it – know it as a fundamental truth!*

*And also know the truth of the feelings in your heart, right in the middle of your breathing . . . all your emotions . . . and also the deeper feelings of the heart where you feel God's presence . . . where Jesus' love lives within you . . . where Spirit indwells – feel it . . . know it!*

*And as your awareness expands to include your whole body here in this present moment, feel yourself as a whole being . . . alive and as real as all the rest of reality . . . that's the thing – you're the truth . . . And so, when you look within, and accept yourself just as you are, in that process of total acceptance of yourself you know the reality of who you really are . . .*

*Then comes a deeper quiet in your mind, in your whole being, as you open your heart to the inflow of wisdom and truth beyond your personal reality . . . breathe into the experience that comes to you when you open to know the truth . . . and allow that knowing to set you free . . . right now . . .*

# ✿ Pause & Experience

# 14

# "Be perfect . . . even as your Father in heaven is perfect"

Finally, we come to the controversial saying of Jesus that takes all this to the ultimate level of completion and wholeness: Be perfect, just as God is perfect. I remember being told as a child that children cannot possibly understand this quote of Jesus, but that we weren't, in the meantime, to think that this meant we were equal to God in any way. I remember being firmly instructed that just the opposite was the case: We are hopelessly imperfect and continually sinking into sin and degradation, especially in our thoughts and the imaginings that come to us.

I actually got to seminary without anyone ever really explaining to me what Jesus meant by these words. Then at seminary, I was told a different story by each professor I asked, not to mention scores of theologians whose books I read on the topic. And as would be expected, the explanations I was given were philo-sophical in nature, head-trippy in content, and utterly meaning-less when it came to my direct confrontation with the words in meditation.

> In meditation, when I quieted my thoughts and simply allowed these words of Jesus to resonate within me, there was always the clear dictum that would arise in my heart, the quiet but certain voice that would say to me, "Just go ahead and do it!"
>
> Again, we have a clear call to action. Jesus didn't say we were to *think about* being perfect. He just said *be perfect.* That's how Jesus' important teachings always hit me – they're not intellectual ideas, they're core-level truths being expressed. And the only way to get into the truth of what Jesus is saying is to – do it.

And so I would, just for a short moment, allow myself to be per-fect. I would let go of all my judgments against myself, and give myself a clean slate – perfect. Nothing wrong with me. I'm okay exactly as I am. Nothing wrong! Everything right!

And as soon as I entered into the first part of the equation Jesus had laid out for me, "Be perfect," the second part of the equation would be activated: I would experience a flash of con-nection with God's perfection. I would suddenly lose my sense of being separate from God. I would be just like God, in harmony, cleansed, purified . . . and oh, my God, what a feeling!

I would then pop out of the meditation, trembling, somehow afraid almost to death that what I'd just done was a mortal sin, totally forbidden. Even though Jesus said to do it, and even though it felt utterly divine and eternally right, my programmed Christian nervous system would react as if lightning were going to strike. Because I'd just dared to assume that I'm as good and pure and powerful and perfect as God. And human beings are not allowed to feel that way – or else.

Or else what?

# Fear of God

The God of the Old Testament was portrayed mostly as a seriously nasty guy who would lay waste entire cities if the inhabitants did something he didn't allow. God was wrathful and people feared his wrath. There's more blood and gore in the Old Testament than almost any other book I've read; and a lot of that blood and gore was the direct result of God's wrath striking out and obliterating human beings for doing what they knew they shouldn't. Without question, one of the things they knew they shouldn't do was to think that they were as good, great, and perfect as God.

So then along came Jesus saying something exactly the opposite; in fact, he encouraged his followers to reverse the tide. He out and out ordered them to be perfect, just exactly as God is perfect. And of course, the experience of being perfect just as God is perfect is no different from experiencing being God. At least I could never see the difference. Perfection is perfection, and when I'm perfect, I'm perfection itself. Within this perfection, there is nothing that separates me from God.

"In the beginning was the Word, and the Word was with God, and the Word was God." So begins the fourth Gospel, according to John. When we become perfect, when we wipe from our minds any self-judgment of imperfection, not only do we come into the presence of God, but we also *are* God. As far as I can see, the only thing that keeps us from living perpetually in this state of perfection is our fear that we'd be doing something wrong if we saw ourselves as perfect.

> Here's the priestly difficulty with this "Be ye therefore perfect" order by Jesus. If you perceive yourself as perfect, then you don't need Jesus to die for your sins, because you're not a sinner. Right there – see it! Jesus is pointing beyond all the "die for my sins" theology, and setting us free.

The truth is that we are perfect; otherwise Jesus wouldn't tell us to be perfect. Our thoughts make us imperfect, yes. Therefore

Jesus orders us to move beyond our ingrained cultural attitudes and negative judgments, and experience the truth. And this truth will surely set us free.

How to move beyond the fear of being perfect? Go ahead and experience yourself as perfect, for just a few breaths at first. Simply say to yourself, "I am perfect," and allow these words to effortlessly resonate throughout your being. Say it . . . do it. And see if God strikes you dead for choosing to tune in to and experience your perfect nature.

More and more, you'll discover in your heart, as the truth of the matter, that God loves you to feel perfect – this is the natural state of unconditional self-love. We are all perfect in love. That's why Jesus brought such focus to "loving ourselves as he loves us," knowing full well that, as he stated, he loves us just as his Father in heaven loves him. The logic is immaculate. It's the truth. Let's live within it . . .

## All Together Now

So you see how this all fits together. Each of the seven statements of Jesus that we've looked into is part of the greater vision of who we are and what our relationship with the divine truly is, if we surrender to reality and participate in this greater spiritual community.

> It's all so simple when we put aside our fears and our assumptions, and begin looking to our hearts and our feelings, and listening to what our inner voice is telling us. Spirit is always waiting to speak the truth to us, if we're quiet and open to listening.

Knowing the truth is all about listening to God's voice, an inner voice which emerges from the center of your heart. And that voice is quietly whispering, "Go ahead and experience who you really are. Experience being perfect – being one with God in love. Let Spirit act through you each new moment – and enjoy living in heaven on Earth."

## "Be perfect . . . even as your Father in heaven is perfect"

At least that's the voice I often hear. Of course, sometimes I forget; I get pulled down into thoughts that separate me from the love of God in my heart. We all seem to regularly lose our conscious sense of connection. We're human after all, and the biological ego function of the ego-mind that tries to run our internal show sometimes pulls us into fear-based thoughts. Our cultural programming so often yanks us out of paradise and into attitudes and beliefs that collapse our spiritual bubble.

But we also have the power to take charge of our minds so that we live more and more in love, and less and less in fear. We have the conscious ability to live in the present moment and let Spirit act through us, rather than living in the past and the future and letting our ego run the show.

We have the choice to accept, surrender, and participate rather than reject, dominate, and manipulate our way through the present moment. I hope that the meditation program you're now going to learn, based on the seven sayings of Jesus that we've just explored, will offer you a solid lifelong path to walk, one that helps you stay in the present moment, in your heart, and one with God.

The choice is always here before us. That's the interior game of life: each moment, seeing to what extent we can continually choose the light. We are God's perfect creation. All thoughts and beliefs to the contrary must go. Let's do it!

# ⚘ Reflection Time

*Do you feel that God's creation is perfect? If God is perfect, how can anything he creates be anything but perfect? If God created you (all manipulative theologies aside), you are indeed perfect. Furthermore, if you do as Jesus said and stop all your judging, how can the idea of imperfection even cross your mind? This is it – God's perfect creation.*

*The air flowing in and out of your nose . . . perfect . . . the movements in your chest and belly as you breathe . . . perfect . . . the feelings in your heart, whatever they are . . . they're perfect . . . "I am perfect . . . I am whole . . . I am one with God."*

*Love comes flowing into your heart . . . and that love is perfect . . . that love heals . . . that love purifies . . . that love is what makes you perfect . . . God is love . . . and when you are full of love, you are full of God . . . that's all there is to it . . . loving . . .*

# ⚘ Pause & Experience

## Part Three

# Experiencing the New Meditation

We now come to the very heart of our exploration: the pragmatic and utterly profound process of opening our hearts and minds to direct communion with the spirit of Jesus in our lives, and beyond into total active oneness with God.

There are seven steps, or expansions, to this New Meditation experience. Each builds on the previous expansion; the order is important. We've already talked about each of these expansions. Now it's time to focus purely on the experience itself, beyond all words and thoughts. To accomplish this, I'll teach you seven meditation phrases that immediately turn your attention toward each new expansion. Then all you do is be quiet, stay aware of your breathing . . . listen to your inner voice . . . and open your heart to the touch of God.

You can move through this seven-phrase expansion process quite rapidly when you have just a few minutes, or take longer when you have more time. Each time you say the meditation phrases in proper order, the unique eliciting power of these phrases will stimulate an ever-expanding awakening. Then in the Final Words section toward the end of this book, I'll teach you the final expansion of the meditation – a truly remarkable way to move through the seven expansions not just once but three or four times, rising higher and higher in the Jesus Spiral, until all thoughts fall away entirely, even the focus phrases, and you enter your unique personal communion with God.

15

# Breathing with Jesus

## *Meditation 1: "God is breathing me."*

Meditation, at heart, means simply being acutely aware in the present moment. Yes, there are all kinds of highly esoteric formats, rituals, and ceremonies for meditating. But the meditation experience itself always comes down to the same basic process: becoming aware of your presence here in this eternal moment, then expanding that personal awareness as it comes more and more into direct intimate contact and communion with the divine.

I want to show you the most simple and powerful meditation process I know for quickly tuning in to your deeper meditative experience. I'm going to present this meditation process entirely within the framework of Jesus' teachings, and his ongoing presence in our hearts.

> Always, meditation begins with the act of turning your awareness toward your breath experience right now. The "breath of God" is a theme and presence throughout the Bible. Yahweh "breathed life" into Adam in the creation scene; and even the name *Yahweh* is translated from the ancient Hebrew as "breath of God."

Breathing is key, especially when you move into meditation and experience how a quiet focus on your own breathing can serve as a direct pathway into your heart. In fact, an encounter with your Creator always awaits you, right in the middle of your own breathing experience.

I've already introduced you to a number of experiences with your breathing, earlier in this book. Let's move again through the basic breath-focus process, because this is the first spiritual habit to establish if you want to expand your sense of connectedness with your higher spiritual nature.

> You don't have to do anything or change anything to begin meditating on your breathing; just expand your awareness right now as you read these words, to include the sensation happening in your nose as the air flows in . . . and the air flows out . . . and the air flows in again.

If you learn nothing more from this book other than how to stay aware – for the rest of your life – of the air flowing in and out of your nose, this will be quite enough. Breathing, as I say in so many of my books, is the beginning and the ending in meditation and personal awakening.

When you're aware of your breathing experience, you know that you're tuned in to the present moment. The simple act of expanding your awareness to include your breath experience shifts you into the kingdom of heaven – amazing! There are entire meditation traditions, especially in Buddhism, where breath awareness is all you do. Through simply holding your attention on your breathing over a period of half an hour to an hour daily, you can indeed transform your life in spiritual directions.

The difficulty is that most people can't sustain this simple meditation, nor make it a habit they do every day. Why? Because, as you know, your thinking mind immediately wants to get all your attention focused back on what it considers the most important things to be aware of – mostly ruminating about the past, worrying about the future, and making mental plans to somehow avoid problems you imagine might happen. Unfortunately, because we encounter Jesus, God, and Spirit only right here as an experience in the present moment, the undereducated ego is constantly pulling us away from our spiritual center, in order to think up a storm in past-future mental functions.

So how do we manage to maintain an awareness of our breathing? I've found more answers to this in perceptual psychological research than in meditative training, so let me share with you the shortcut to breath awareness.

## The Nose Knows

First of all, you need to consciously redirect your power of attention toward the actual experience of the air flowing in and out of your nose. This instantly shifts you into the present moment, into perception mode, and at least somewhat out of thinking mode. You've made one step toward entering into God's presence.

Do it now if you want – feel that sensation! You'll notice that the sensation is (usually) stronger when you inhale than when you exhale, because of the air temperature differential on the inhalation. Usually the air flowing into your nose is cooler than your body temperature, so there's a distinct sensation based on temperature difference, along with the movement sensations and scents in the air.

For one to three breaths, I want you to hold your full attention on your nose and what you're feeling inside your nose, as you inhale and exhale. Feel that rather sharp sensation of the cool air flowing into your nose . . . and then the less intense, warmer air flowing out on the exhale . . . and notice what you feel as you inhale again now . . .

But before you get bored with doing that one seemingly simplistic thing and go back to thinking, I encourage you to go ahead and make the next step toward God: Expand your mind's attention to include, along with the sensations in your nose while breathing, the sensations of movement in your chest and belly being generated by your inhalations and exhalations.

> Practice this until you get good at holding in your awareness two different sensations at the same time: the sensations in your nose as you breathe, and the sensations in your chest and belly as you breathe. This act of being aware of two different bodily sensations at the same time, in and of itself, has been proven to rapidly quiet all thoughts.

It's very hard to be lost in thought and, at the same time, immersed in sensation. So in this breath-expansion process, you consciously choose to shift from thinking to experiencing. At first, this might take a bit of practice. Please stay with it until you learn it by heart; master this shift into full-harmony breath awareness. Do your best never to let go of this new mental tool for shifting from past-future thinking into present-moment experiencing. This is the heart of meditation; this is where you encounter the divine. Right here, right now, right in the middle of your breath experience.

We speak of being inspired. Long ago, *inspire* meant "to inhale," just as *expire* meant "to exhale." When we are focused on the air flowing into our bodies, insights also seem to come flowing into our minds – because we've quieted our mundane thoughts and opened up to a higher level of understanding. I've already written full books on this (*Quiet Your Mind*, especially), so I'm not going to wax eloquent about the vast benefits of being aware of your breathing. Simply said, the spiritual aim is to be here in the present moment as much as you can. And breath awareness is the direct path to accomplishing this goal.

> For concrete help in learning to tune in to your breathing, please take the time to memorize the following twin focus phrases that I teach in all my meditation books: "I'm aware of the air flowing in and out of my nose," and "I'm also aware of the movements in my chest and belly as I breathe."

There's great power in saying these words to yourself as you tune in to your breathing. The verbal statements will instantly help you do just what you said. So learn these focus phrases by heart. Use them often each day to help you shift into God's country.

## The Eternal Atmosphere

As you tune in to your own breathing experience, you will also naturally tune in to the air around you that you're breathing. In this way you will naturally expand your consciousness beyond your personal awareness bubble, out into the atmosphere that surrounds our entire planet as one continuous whole gaseous ocean.

This atmospheric ocean is made up of the same molecules of air that existed thousands, millions, even billions of years ago. There is nothing gained nor lost in the universe, and the oxygen you bring into your lungs and bloodstream and then use to light your inner fire consists of the exact same oxygen molecules people were breathing long, long ago.

> In fact, statistically speaking, Jesus most surely breathed some of the same air molecules you're breathing right now – so we have even this physiological link with Jesus in breath meditation.

Meanwhile here you are right now, still breathing . . . and step by step learning to stay aware of your breathing more and more, even while you do whatever else you're doing at the moment. The trick lies in the core process of consciousness expansion, of becoming aware of more at once than you habitually do. Spirituality is all about consciousness expansion. You don't contract your awareness in order to experience God's presence in your life – you expand your awareness. At least in the type of meditation I teach, you don't lose awareness of your individual identity in order to experience God. You stay aware of your individual breathing, your personal heartbeat, your whole body here in the present moment – and, at the same time, you expand your awareness to also include God's presence. All in one and one in all.

# Reflection Time

*Experience this breath meditation again . . . the air flowing in . . . the air flowing out . . . your heart right in the middle of your breathing . . . and the feeling in your whole body . . . be conscious of your entire presence at once . . . and now, expand your personal awareness to include the air around you . . . the whole world . . . and in the midst of all this earthly experience, also tune in to the infinite spiritual presence of Jesus, of all the spiritual masters . . . and within this infinite expansion, enjoy your personal experience of merging with the divine . . .*

# Pause & Experience

## Consider the Lilies – Again

So many people feel that life is an effort, that they have to push through every new moment and force their way to survive and get what they want. People even think that breathing is something they make happen – and that every breath is an effort. Jesus taught just the opposite.

When we consider the lilies, we see that they do not make an effort. Yet everything they need comes to them. Most of nature seems to make no effort – but we do. We tend to continually struggle, push, and force our way through life, provoked by anxieties, fear-based aggressions, and old attitudes that generate tension and struggle.

Put bluntly, what a drag. Especially since the spiritual path is an effortless flow. Jesus told us to consider the lilies and live our lives in harmony with the insight that the lilies offer about God's creation. And nowhere is this more important than with your breathing. I recommend when you first tune in to your breath experience (which will probably feel tight rather than relaxed), that instead of trying to change your breathing at all, simply accept your breathing – and set your breathing free.

This is actually quite easy to do. As you become aware of the air flowing in and out of your nose, and expand to include the movements in your chest and belly with each breath, purposefully exhale all the way to empty. Then, for just five to ten seconds, hold your breath. Make contact with that powerful inner force that keeps you breathing. Then when you're good and hungry for air (but not so long that it's uncomfortable), go ahead and let that next beautiful inhale come rushing into your lungs – without any effort at all!

Do this "exhale-hold-inhale" routine two to five times in a row, until your new inhales are entirely without effort, and feel delicious! You are now living like the lilies, making zero effort to breathe. Instead, you're letting God breathe you. And you are breathing with God.

To bring this experience fully into focus, you can say to

yourself as the primary meditation phrase of this first expansion: *"God is breathing me."*

This is such a wonderful gift to give yourself many times a day, and it only takes one minute to do. Furthermore it moves you into position for the next expansions of the full meditation. Here is the first expansion in a nutshell so that you can memorize it over the next few weeks, and make it your permanent instant gateway into heaven on earth.

# ❦ Meditation Expansion 1:
## "God is breathing me."

*This first expansion can be done on its own, or as the beginning of the full New Meditation experience. If you want some audio guidance for learning this process, you can also go online (www.johnselby.com) and I'll guide you with my voice.*

*Just relax and get comfortable . . . stretch a moment if you want . . . yawn to relax further . . . now turn your mind's full attention toward your nose, to the sensation of the air flowing in and out of your nose with each inhale and exhale . . . and say: "I'm aware of the air flowing in and out of my nose."*

*Now expand your awareness to also include the movements in your chest and belly as you breathe . . . say, "I also feel the movements in my chest and belly."*

*On your next exhale, push all the air out and hold on empty a few moments . . . get hungry for air . . . then relax and let your next inhale come rushing in through your nose all on its own! Do this two to five times, to set your breathing free.*

*Now allow your awareness to expand to include the air around you, which you're breathing . . . expand to be aware of the unifying atmosphere of the Earth in which you're immersed right now . . . along with all of us together . . .*

*Now expand your awareness to include the presence of Spirit, and the Creator of all this earthly life . . . and as you open to a new experience, say to yourself, "God is breathing me."*

#  Pause & Experience

<h1>16</h1>

<h1>Entering the Kingdom</h1>

## Meditation 2: "I let go of the past and future, and embrace this eternal moment."

You are in the process of establishing an ongoing primary awareness of your breathing experience. You're also ready to learn six special meditation phrases based on Jesus' meditative suggestions, which will direct your attention toward primal experiences. Please hold in mind, as you spend a few weeks now training to master this unique meditation process, that the process only works if you continue to remain aware of your breathing throughout.

> In this meditation, whenever you lose awareness of your breathing, please return to the first step, move through the process of regaining full awareness of your breath-

ing – and then continue again through the following six steps.

We've talked about how love, insight, and inspiration manifest in our hearts and minds only in the present moment. The historic past is nothing more than fragments of memories and story lines of our historians. The future is nothing but a possible scenario. The present moment is the only place where we actually experience anything. This is it. And in this second expansion, I offer you a very powerful focus phrase, which will instantly and fully shift your mind's attention to the eternally unfolding present moment: *"I let go of the past and future, and embrace this eternal moment."*

When you say these words quietly to yourself (without any sound), at some level they instantly manifest the intent you've stated. That's the power of focus phrases when they are worded properly for maximum effect. Please note that when you come to a focus phrase that has a comma or a dash in the middle of the sentence, you will want to say the first part of the sentence on one exhalation and then allow those words ("I let go of the past and the future . . .") to resonate throughout your being as you inhale. Letting go – this is an experience! Then you are ready to say on your next exhale, the real punch line: "and embrace this eternal moment."

I assure you I've chosen these words with extreme care. In fact, what else can we do than embrace the eternal now? With open arms, we bring God's new moment of creation into our senses and hearts – that's how we enter the kingdom of heaven on Earth.

## Embracing the New

Let me bring an often-used but essential metaphor into play here. You can't have your hand grasping one thing and at the same time reach out and grasp a new thing. You can't be embracing the past and the future (lost in thoughts, memories, and imaginings) and, at the same time, open up and embrace the present moment. Life just doesn't work that way. There must be a letting go for there to be a receiving of the new. That's why this focus phrase is stated exactly as it is: "I let go of the past and the future, and embrace this eternal moment."

Please don't bother overmuch with thinking about what "this eternal moment" means as an idea. We're talking pure experience here: the actual sensations of the air flowing in and out of your nose or mouth . . . the movements in your chest and belly as you breathe . . . your whole-body presence in the here and now . . . the sounds around you . . . what you see, what you smell, what you taste . . . and as you expand a step deeper into reality, what inner feelings and experiences, insights and decisions come directly to you from your spiritual core of being.

Each moment, you are continually letting go of the past in order to remain in the present moment. It's so easy to have an experience, and then immediately start thinking about that experience and what that experience reminds you of.

> Out of habit, we continually let go of the present moment as we drop into thought. I'm encouraging you to begin developing the inner mental strength and habit of continually letting go of thought, so that you can stay in the present moment.

This second step is as vital as the first step for moving deeper and deeper into direct communion with Jesus and God. This is the statement of intent that opens the gate to the kingdom.

## The Ego King

As we advance through this book, I want to offer you the shortest and simplest framework for taking this meditation process into your heart and making it your own. Ultimately, it's your personality's ego function that will serve as your pragmatic step-by-step guide through this meditation process each new time you do it. Contrary to many traditional meditation traditions, this new method does not in any way try to shut out or silence your ego. Instead, we're giving your ego something vital to do right in the middle of the meditation experience. After all, it's your ego that's going to remember to do this meditation each new day, and then remember each of the seven focus phrases in proper order, and say them.

Once the clear value of this primal mental exercise is understood, the ego function of the mind is not going to fight against your deeper spiritual awakening. As your logical mind realizes that it's to your survival advantage to live more in the here and now and be guided by your inner voice of wisdom and spiritual directive, the ego will rise like a champion and regularly walk you through this process.

In fact, I'm purposefully writing much of this book speaking honestly to your ego, to your personality self, to your survival function, which determines what you focus on each new moment. And the task at hand is not difficult: All your ego function needs to do is memorize the seven focus phrases I'm now teaching you. It's that simple – and purposefully so.

We need to get quickly beyond words, structure, and concepts. Therefore the fewer words the better. Without this basic seven-step verbal structure, however, people tend to get rapidly sucked back into normal thinking habits and not move into meditation at all. So I offer you this method as a basic ego word-bridge into pure spiritual experience. Your ego rules your attention, so let's give the ruler something important to do!

## Eternity

Here's another great paradox. In our everyday assumptions about time, each new moment lasts only a very short time. In fact, in reality, there is no time at all to be experienced in the present moment. Do you notice a marker between one moment and the next in your experience? Where does this moment end, and the next moment begin? Sequential linear time flow, when studied carefully, is nothing more than a concept itself, a handy creation of the human mind that enables us to reflect and think about the past. You'll begin to discover this for yourself the more you meditate.

As cognitive scientists (and the ancient meditation masters as well) tell us, we have two mental modes for experiencing the flow of time. In the most common mode, we live in the handy illusion that seconds, moments, and minutes are going by, one after the other. The thinking mind functions in this past-present-future paradigm, and so it imposes this grid on our experience of the present moment.

But you know from experience that quite often you slip out of this regimented march of seconds and minutes into a most curious and enjoyable state of mind, where time disappears and you're fully engrossed in what seems to be an eternal present moment where you don't notice time going by at all.

This is the creative mind-state, this is the pleasure mind-state, this is the meditative mind-state. When you're totally immersed in the present moment, there is no time at all. And this is what is called eternal time. Your experience is the center of time, and time radiates outward from you in all directions. You are moving in the flow of eternal time to where you don't notice the movement at all – you are a part of it.

This sense of eternal time comes into being when you say to yourself, "I let go of the past and the future, and embrace this eternal moment." These words point you toward the modality in your mind where, indeed, you're living in eternity. If you want to know what the spiritual state of mind is, this is it. Because in this eternal state of mind, you are plugged directly in to the entirety of life – you are not separate from the infinite. You are here now in the kingdom of heaven that never ends.

Eternal life isn't found in the future. Eternal life is found only in the here and now of the present moment. And all you need to do to enter is to remember to turn your mind's attention in the direction of the eternal moment by saying one magical meditation phrase to yourself so often that this eternal quality of consciousness becomes your new habitual state of consciousness.

# Meditation Expansion 2:
## "I let go of the past and future, and embrace this eternal moment."

*For your ego's direct memorization and your deeper self's effortless expansion, let me lay out in shorthand the basic flow of the first and the second meditation expansions. I'll then keep adding to this meditation formula as we bring new focus phrases into the process, until you have before you the full seven-step meditation. You might want to write down these seven sentences a few times to encourage easy memorization. Also bear in mind that you can go to my website and listen to my voice guiding you through the process, as an effortless way to memorize the meditation by internalizing my voice:*

*Get comfortable, stretch if you want and yawn to relax further . . . Turn your mind's full attention to the sensation of the air flowing in and out of your nose . . . Expand your awareness to include the movements in your chest and belly . . . Exhale – hold – and then let your next inhale come flowing in . . . Say to yourself, "God is breathing me."*

*Expand your awareness to include your whole body here in this present moment, as you tune in to all your senses – sight, sound, smell, touch, taste . . . Say: "I let go of the past and future, and embrace this eternal moment."*

*And now just breathe into this expanded always-new experience of the here and now . . . and if you want, go back and say these two meditation phrases again to yourself, to allow the words to take you deeper . . .*

 # Pause & Experience

# 17

# Surrendering to
# the Higher Good

## Meditation 3: "I surrender my
## will to the higher good."

The first two steps in the New Meditation process involve the usual ego function of the mind taking steps to shift attention toward direct experience in the present moment. We now come to the third step, where the ego directly states its intent to relinquish, at least temporarily, its usual ego manipulations and self-centered plotting and planning in favor of something greater.

This third expansion is potentially gigantic; every time you say these words and move through this step, you'll advance

your mental ability to shift your attention toward participating in "the higher good."

As before, you'll say this meditation phrase with a quiet inner
voice that you feel in your vocal cords, tongue, and lips as slight
movement and hear inside yourself, but which doesn't involve
the flow of air out of your mouth. You'll experience the flow of
air out of your nose and movements in your vocalizing muscles as
you say the sentence to yourself, but without audible sound. In
this way, you "hear" yourself talking, you feel yourself talking, you
experience the power of the words, but you're talking for inner
hearing, not outer communication.

## The Power of Surrender

In a couple of pages, we'll explore the concept of your individual
will and the higher good, but first let's see how the words of this
expansion spontaneously affect you. Go ahead and say the following focus phrase a few times. Don't go off into thought. Stay with
the emerging feelings in your heart and body; see how the words
impact you directly.

# Pause and Reflect

*Tune in to your breathing, and on your next exhale say:*
"I surrender my will to the higher good."
*Inhale quietly . . . and again say . . .*
"I surrender my will to the higher good."
*And again . . . inhale, and then say:*
"I surrender my will to the higher good."
*Take a bit of time off now, put down the book . . . close your eyes perhaps . . . say the focus phrase another time or two . . . and as you remain aware of your breathing, see what experience comes to you as you explore the power and majesty of your ego self surrendering to your greater self . . .*

# Pause & Experience

## Transpersonal Consciousness

What is the higher will, the higher good? Again, I've chosen my words very carefully after years of exploration and experimentation with focus phrases. "The higher good" is a perfect term because it doesn't reflect any particular theology or belief system; it simply points our attention toward the universal spiritual reality that we have all experienced one way or another in our hearts and souls.

> We are most of the time experiencing life from within our personal consciousness, our individual and often quite selfish and contracted ego bubble. But we are also capable of expanding this bubble of awareness beyond our usual ego buzz, and surrendering to a higher, wiser, even spiritually transpersonal level of consciousness.

This expanded reality that lies beyond all our individual strivings and concepts perceives the whole; in fact it *is* the whole – it's the consciousness of the Creator. And its will definitely reflects the greater good. Jesus stated for himself, and equally for all of us, the wise stance: "Not my will, but Thine." Even when close to death, Jesus the man spoke to God directly, and surrendered his personal ego will (which wants to stay alive) to the will of his transpersonal wisdom and spiritual guidance.

My experience is that only when my ego consciously takes this step of surrendering to the higher good do I expand into spiritual experience. Only through surrender do we know God.

There is a higher will, and we must choose which we want to let direct our lives. We cannot embrace spiritual guidance while at the same time gripping ego directives. That's the nature of this third expansion, and this third choice. In the first expansion, we choose to turn our mind's attention to our breath experience. In the second expansion, we choose to turn our mind's attention to the present moment. And in this third expansion, we choose to focus on participating in the greater good, as we let go of our ego control and surrender to a higher guidance.

Is this something you want to do? Perhaps your ego, your individual personality, doesn't want to surrender to higher guidance. I'm not insisting that you do this; all I'm suggesting is that you experiment with the feeling and experience that come when you say the focus phrase, and see what happens. And again, only when you move through this process a number of times will the real power and change happen. For now, just play with this, be a consciousness explorer. See what comes to you.

#  Meditation Expansion 3:
## "I surrender my will to the higher good."

*Again, here's the flow of the meditation, this time through three expansions:*

*Get comfortable, stretch a moment if you want and yawn to relax further . . .*

*Turn your mind's full attention to the air flowing in and out of your nose . . .*

*Expand your awareness to include the movements in your chest and belly . . .*

*Exhale – hold – and then let your next inhale come flowing effortlessly in . . .*

*Say to yourself, "God is breathing me."*

*Expand your awareness to include your whole body here in this present moment, as you tune in to all your senses – sight, sound, smell, touch, taste . . .*

*Say: "I let go of the past and the future, and embrace this eternal moment."*

*Breathe into this expanded always-new experience of the here and now . . . and say to yourself, "I surrender my will to the higher good."*

*Allow your awareness to expand as you experience in your heart the merger of your personal will and the greater will . . . the greater good!*

# Pause & Experience

# 18

# Opening Your Heart

## Meditation 4: "I open my heart to receive God's love."

Only now in this fourth step, after moving through the first three expansions, is your ego ready to let go of its dominance, and allow your heart to open and experience the inflow of God's love. I hope you see the essential progressive nature of this meditation. Much of this process is based on pragmatic psychological analysis of how the mind works, how the ego functions, and how the ego can choose, in the proper setting, to relinquish control to a higher guidance.

> Only by moving through the first three expansions and honoring the wisdom of the ego's decisions can we reach the point where the ego is ready to choose to let go of ego

control and enter into a higher level of mental and spiritual functioning.

I've written often about the need for mind management and consciousness management, and this is what we're accomplishing in the first three expansions of this meditation process. We're managing our ego minds in such a way as to transcend ego control. That's the big hurdle in all meditation. This basic process I'm guiding you through accomplishes that primary goal in a predictable, enjoyable, and successful way.

Now we're ready in the fourth expansion to actually go for it: to declare what we really want to have happen in our meditation. I've explored many focus phrases on this general theme of opening up to experience God directly, and found that it's essential to state exactly what you want. Opening to receive God's love is primarily an experience of the heart. Therefore we need to directly encourage our hearts to open. If we don't overtly and regularly say to ourselves, "I open my heart," then our hearts are probably going to remain mostly closed. That's the reality we face.

> Our ego habit is to keep our hearts protectively closed so that we're not hurt or overwhelmed by outside forces. It's now time to take the leap of faith, open up in trust, and state our intent to experience the inflow of God's love into our hearts.

"I open my heart to receive God's love." We are now focusing our attention not in the direction of a concept or idea (God), but toward a power and an experience (God's love). One of the key points in Jesus' teachings is that he focuses our attention over and over on love itself, the experience, the flow, the power and the glory of God's love. Our minds will always try to settle in and "think about" the word "God"; the word is such an ingrained elicitor of theological thoughts. But when we focus not on God, but on the expression of God's presence through his infinite unconditional power of love, we tune directly into *the feeling of God's presence* in our hearts.

All you have to do is say the focus phrase and your mind will turn its attention directly toward the reality that is emerging right now, in your heart, as you choose to experience the inflow of God's love into your life. This is a brave, exciting, magnificent action you take, each time you do this meditation. So go ahead and explore how it feels in your throat, your lungs, your tongue, and your heart when you say the following words.

---

# ✣ Pause and Reflect

"I open my heart to receive God's love."

*Inhale quietly . . . and again say,*

"I open my heart to receive God's love."

*And again . . . inhale, and then say,*

"I open my heart to receive God's love."

*Take a bit of time now, put down the book, close your eyes perhaps . . . say the focus phrase another time or two . . . and as you remain aware of your breathing, see what experience comes as you explore the always-new feeling of God's love flowing into your heart . . .*

# ❧ Pause & Experience

---

## Love – The Experience

At this point in the meditation, many people tend to lose awareness of their breathing. Instead they slip into thought. Especially if a strong experience comes into your heart at this moment of opening to the divine, your mind might instantly want to process the experience by thinking about it. Unfortunately, as soon as you start to think about an experience you just had, you lose the ongoing experience itself! This is the downside of the thinking mind. We lose the experience when we start to reflect on the experience.

I'm not saying that reflection is bad, certainly not. But for the total potential expansion of the full meditation process we're learning here, you'll want to master this fine art of remaining tuned in to your breathing – that's your experiential ballast. That's what keeps your thoughts temporarily quiet so that the experience can continue.

Even right now, notice if you're still aware of your breathing as you continue reading . . . and if not, gently return your attention to your breathing and present-moment experience by saying again the secular mantra:

"I feel the air flowing in and out of my nose."
"I also feel the movements in my chest and belly as I breathe."
"I'm aware of my whole body, here in this present moment."

Only by returning again and again to these three statements and bringing your awareness to full present-moment focus do you place your attention where you can experience God's love flowing into your heart. Otherwise you'll mostly get stuck thinking about God's love, rather than experiencing it.

What I find most remarkable, and also most tragic from a certain perspective, is that God does not push into our lives. We have the power to close our hearts to God's love. Our culture mostly conditions us to maintain this fear-based stance of a closed heart. Even after two thousand years, as a culture, we still haven't quite gotten the point of Jesus' teachings. That realization was one of the reasons I broke with the established Christian heritage – it simply hasn't gotten the job done. Somehow we must unite psychology (how the mind works) and spirituality (how we open to God's love) so that the psychological conditioning we all receive no longer stands between God's love and us. I sincerely hope that this book carries the power to help you make this leap. And this fourth expansion is the proof of the pudding.

## Ever Onward

So often, people come to this fourth expansion and feel nothing at all happening in their hearts. This will probably happen to you at times. It happens to me at times. What do you do when you say, "I open my heart to receive God's love," and you don't seem to be receiving anything at all? This is a crucial point in your meditative life. If you immediately judge yourself, or judge the process, as no good, as a failure, you'll suffer an immense setback.

> Please, right at this point, don't be bothered if you feel nothing in your heart. Just say the sentence "I open my heart to receive God's love," breathe into whatever experience (or lack thereof) comes to you, and then move right on to the next, the fifth, expansion, without letting go of your awareness of your breathing, and the step-by-step progression of the meditation.

Trust me here. There are dynamics in this seven-step meditation that are not visible but are in operation nonetheless. I have a deeper game plan here, for making sure that this meditation technique is a long-term success in your life. That's my responsibility, and I have definitely taken that responsibility with all seriousness over the years I've developed this meditation process. There's more to come – and you're in process here. Even if you have a deep experience as you open your heart to God's love, even then, please continue with the meditation. The final three expansions will take the experience you've had thus far and expand it even further.

For now, let's sum up the first four expansions in a format you can begin memorizing day by day.

# ❦ Meditation Expansion 4:
## "I open my heart to receive God's love."

*Here's the flow of the meditation through the first four expansions. See how much of this you now know by heart and what you still have to memorize.*

*Get comfortable, stretch a moment if you want, and yawn to relax further . . .*

*Turn your mind's full attention to the air flowing in and out of your nose . . .*

*Expand your awareness to include the movements in your chest and belly . . .*

*Exhale – hold – and then let your next inhale flow effortlessly in . . . Say to yourself, "God is breathing me."*

*Expand your awareness to include your whole body here in this present moment, as you tune in to all your senses – sight, sound, smell, touch, taste . . .*

*Say: "I let go of the past and the future, and embrace this eternal moment."*

*Breathe into this expanded always-new experience of the here and now . . . and say to yourself, "I surrender my will to the higher good."*

*Now turn your focus of attention to the feelings in your heart, right in the middle of your breathing experience, and say to yourself, "I open my heart to receive God's love."*

#  Pause & Experience

# 19

# Listening to Spirit

## Meditation 5: "I am quiet . . . and listening."

You have now, in the first four expansions: (1) tuned in to your
breathing and whole-body presence in the eternal now, (2) let go
of the past and the future so you can immerse your awareness in
the present moment where Spirit indwells in human life, (3) surrendered your personal ego direction to the higher spiritual
direction of God's guidance in your life, and (4) consciously
opened your heart to receive the inflow of God's love.

These first four steps help set you temporarily free of all the
usual psychological and cultural veils, so that you are beyond
thoughts and beliefs and ready to engage fully with whatever spiritual insights and empowerment this new moment has to offer
you.

Now it's time to take the final leap and shift fully, entirely into "receive mode" as you say to yourself, *"I am quiet . . . and listening."*

After you practice and master this meditative process, the impact of these five seemingly simple words can be both immediate and immense. You will do best to say the words to yourself on two breaths, first saying "I am quiet," and experiencing this deep state on your next inhalation, then saying "and listening," so that your entire being becomes receptive.

What's absolutely key right at this point is to remain aware of your breathing as your ballast – this is your primal grounding in the present moment. Spirit comes on the wings of your breathing. And it's always right in the middle of your breathing experience that the voice of God is heard.

Furthermore, as you've already learned, when you're aware of your breathing, you're also aware of the feelings in your heart, found in the middle of your breathing. You can't separate breath and heart – they're a unified experience. In the fourth expansion, you focused deeply on your heart as love flowed in. Now in the fifth expansion, you remain in this heart-breath focus and expand into a deeper quality of inner listening, of fine attunement to whatever new insight, revelation, feeling, or subtle shifting of your consciousness Spirit might bring you.

Often you will come to the fifth expansion and simply be in a state of inner peace, even bliss. Much of the emotional healing process that comes in this fifth expansion happens without you even noticing specifics – you simply experience the power of God's touch healing, bringing calm where there was upset, love where there was anger, joy where there was sadness.

In this fifth expansion, you surrender not only to God's will in your life, but also to God's healing grace. And as with all deep meditative experiences, you don't "do" anything except dwell in the love of God, and trust God's wisdom and infinite knowing to act within your heart, to heal, inspire, reveal, or whatever.

## Your Inner Voice

Beyond the healing power of this meditation lies the insight dimension, where you are able to tap effortlessly into your own eternal wisdom, which emerges from a source beyond your ego mind, yet finds its way into your everyday consciousness through a verbal sense of knowing and realization. All too often, people pray by constantly talking to God, as I mentioned before. In this fifth step, you say words ("I am quiet . . . and listening") that directly shift your mind into "receive mode," so that you can indeed receive guidance and realization from the divine.

> When you are quiet, and listening, without any cognitive activity to jam your inner airwaves, you will sometimes suddenly hear an inner voice that speaks to you and communicates an answer to questions and difficulties you've been struggling to resolve without previous success.

Some people hear a voice speaking to them inside their minds. Some people talk about God speaking directly to them. Other people have insights pop into their minds from nowhere, or entire realizations, inventions, or other valuable insights instantly appear in their minds. First, the insight event happens, then we try to explain what that event was all about; naturally, each of us has our own assumptions about the source of insight and realization.

What's important isn't your intellectualization about the source of your sudden flash of insight during meditation. What's important is regularly quieting your mind, saying "I am quiet . . . and listening," and, in fact, doing just that: breathing quietly in meditation with your mind at peace, and being receptive to whatever comes to you in whatever form. Some people experience visions, some people see mathematical equations, some people hear angels singing. Whatever comes to you, wonderful. But don't get hung up on explanations of how it happens. Just move regularly into meditation, and open up again!

## Insight, Psychosis, or Vision

Most of us, as we were growing up, had visions and wild inner experiences of many kinds. From birth to around the age of four or five, the interior world of children seems to be rampant with amazing experiences. Then around five or six, we realize that people might consider us crazy if they knew what wild things we were experiencing inside our minds. Out of fear of being treated as crazy, we begin to ignore, push out, forget, and otherwise rid ourselves of all experiences that don't seem to fit the "sanity" norm.

You might find, while meditating and quieting your mind, that those old fears arise again, telling you that it's crazy to quiet your mind and listen, that you're liable to slip back into all those old crazy experiences that you learned to shut out from consciousness so that you'd fit into society and not be rejected. Why risk that again, with this meditation thing?

I personally have never known anyone who meditated and, through meditating, went crazy. I have known loads of people who became more sane through meditating and overcame neurotic and even psychotic tendencies. Meditation is the process of opening up and observing what reality is all about. That's the best definition I know of a sane person: someone who fully embraces reality.

So you don't have to be afraid of going crazy when you set your mind free. Unconditional love and spiritual awakening don't drive you crazy – they heal you emotionally and mentally. Yes, sometimes you'll listen and be receptive in meditation, and experience amazing things. Your role is to breathe into these experiences; don't get attached to them. Just watch them go by. Again, your breathing is your ballast. As long as you're aware of your breathing and your heart, you'll be opening to experiences that will nurture you.

And what about insights? Where do these really come from – beyond our physical minds or just from the creative intuitive part of our brains? Again, this is a question that perhaps science will answer in the next 50 years or so. The underlying issue is whether experimental science can ever prove that there is consciousness and intelligence beyond the brain. Already, with the remarkable findings of the Princeton Engineering Anomalies Research program (www.princeton.edu/~pear/), there is concrete proof that the human mind has the power to reach out beyond the physical body and influence the physical world. Insights do seem to have the ability to come to us from a transpersonal source. And as you'll find in meditation, that term "transpersonal" takes us ultimately to God and infinite wisdom and insight.

> I find it best when meditating, and listening with my mind quiet, simply to be thankful for whatever comes. Often what comes is a deep sense of peace and contentment without any great flashing shows of insight or inner realization.

The purpose of meditation isn't necessarily to gain a result or have something dramatic happen. The purpose of meditation is simply to be quiet, to tune in to your experience in the present moment, and allow that experience to expand as your consciousness expands. What actually happens . . . well, that's always new.

I think I won't say anything further at this point. We're moving deeper into that inner quality of consciousness where all words fall away and God's voice is often heard, or one experiences the touch of Spirit or the guidance of Jesus' presence. And right in the midst of this fifth expansion, of course, you'll find the sixth expansion comes into being.

So let's quickly review the five steps in this new meditation, the Jesus Spiral, that you've now learned or are in the process of memorizing.

# ✿ Meditation Expansion 5:
## "I am quiet . . . and listening."

*Get comfortable, stretch a moment if you want, and yawn to relax further . . . Turn your mind's full attention to the air flowing in and out of your nose . . .*

*Expand your awareness to include the movements in your chest and belly . . . Exhale – hold – and then let your next inhale flow effortlessly in . . .*

*1) Say to yourself, "God is breathing me."*

*Expand your awareness to include your whole body here in this present moment, as you tune in to all your senses – sight, sound, smell, touch, taste . . .*

*2) Say: "I let go of the past and the future, and embrace this eternal moment."*

*Breathe into this expanded always-new experience of the here and now . . .*

*3) Say: "I surrender my will to the higher good."*

*And now turn your focus to the feelings in your heart, right in the middle of your breathing experience.*

*4) Say: "I open my heart to receive God's love."*

*And as you stay aware of your breathing and your heart, expand another step by saying:*

*5) "I am quiet . . . and listening."*

# ✿ Pause & Experience

**20**

# Communing with Jesus

## Meditation 6: "I feel Jesus' presence in my heart."

The term "communion" is a word that the traditional Christian Church uses quite differently than I do. For quite some time, I didn't use the word at all, because of all the old-time connotations.

> But recently, more and more, this term "communion" rises up in my own meditation, because more than any other word in our language, it best expresses the level of personal intimacy and oneness with Jesus' living presence that we can move into, in our meditation experience.

In the traditional Communion ceremony, priests led us through a highly symbolic sacrifice ritual with origins in several ancient religious traditions. The basic theme was that God is sacrificing his only human child, in order to appease – himself, I guess. And in this act of human sacrifice, symbolically, all our own sins and sinful nature are wiped away – once again.

As mentioned earlier, even as a child I found the actual experience of Christian Communion seriously depressive and repulsive. Here was a minister telling me that God had to sacrifice his own son through a most violent and bloody crucifixion for the specific reason that I was such a hopeless sinner. Not only was it my fault that Jesus got murdered, but every Communion Sunday I was also forced to imagine I was eating Jesus' flesh and drinking his blood in order to receive the forgiveness of God the Father. Wow.

In my humble understanding, Spirit led me away from this particular approach to ritual-sacrifice communion with Jesus. I found more and more that when I became quiet in deep prayer at church, and opened to insight regarding my repulsion for the church's priestly blood-sacrifice ceremony, I would suddenly feel Jesus in my heart – without having to participate in the traditional communion ritual.

Being a good boy, I continued moving through the ritual at church for a number of years. But when I got to seminary, I found that quite a number of the seminary students felt as I did. We began letting go of the outer formal communion ceremony and moving instead into group meditation together, simply opening our hearts to experiencing communion with Jesus with zero symbols or sacrifice dimensions.

I would like to share this process with you as we move into the sixth expansion and say words that specifically encourage a deeper heart-to-heart sense of communing with Jesus – beyond all theologies and beliefs. In this sixth expansion, we're ready to consciously open our hearts and minds and experience the presence of Jesus directly at the center of our being.

Again, I mention that breathing and heart awareness are essential to maintain because, in my understanding, Jesus' presence is experienced first as a feeling of a spiritual presence, then as an inner knowing – a sudden awakening leading to full communion beyond all ideas and rituals. And it's always new; the experience is never the same. Each time we enter into meditation and open our hearts and minds to Jesus' presence, we will encounter the next immediate unfolding of our spiritual lives.

As mentioned before, as you commune with Jesus, the experience often expands and you might (if your heart is open) find a female spiritual quality also present in your heart. Sometimes this presence is experienced as Maria Magdalena, sometimes as Mother Mary, sometimes . . .

> Your unique spiritual experience is just that – uniquely yours. I've found it best not to slip in any way into labeling the presence. Simply experience what comes, as you encounter deeper and deeper layers of your own spiritual core, and approach the infinite reality . . . the total God experience transcending all words.

You will find that when you come to this sixth expansion, you will sometimes say, *"I feel Jesus' presence in my heart."* At other times, out of the silence of the fifth expansion, you will find yourself saying, *"I feel Maria's presence in my heart."* Often I find myself saying, *"I feel Spirit's presence in my heart."* And sometimes my deeper voice, speaking from my depths and experiencing what is coming to me in my heart says, *"I feel God's presence in my heart."*

We are in a very deep meditative state at this sixth expansion, and the voice that is saying the focus phrase is often your own deeper voice of wisdom and knowing. There are times when I move through the fifth expansion, *"I am quiet . . . and listening,"* and all sorts of experiences come to me – and when I come to the sixth expansion, the voice speaking becomes speechless, beyond all words. The sixth expansion is really totally up to God. Often you'll say, *"I feel Jesus' presence in my heart."* This is the basic flow of the Jesus Spiral meditation, after all. But I just want to make sure that you feel perfectly free, with the sixth focus phrase, to express what indeed you *do* find in your heart!

The sixth expansion is actually the final expansion of this meditation process. The seventh focus phrase is designed to begin to move you out of the meditation in a gentle, integrative fashion that brings the experiences you've had into a framework you can integrate into your more everyday consciousness and actions, as you begin to emerge from meditation proper into meditation in action.

> This sixth expansion is ultimately "it," in that it's the expansion that takes you all the way . . . and you can dwell within this sixth expansion, and wherever it takes you, for as long as you want.

Here is the whole flow now, for you to continue to memorize. And hold in mind that if you want further help in mastering this meditation, just go online and let me guide you through the process until it becomes a new enduring dimension of your inner experience.

#  Meditation Expansion 6:
## "I feel Jesus' presence in my heart."

*Get comfortable . . . and turn your mind's full attention to the air flowing in and out of your nose . . . Expand your awareness to include the movements in your chest and belly . . . Exhale – hold – and then let your next inhale flow effortlessly in . . .*

*1) Say to yourself, "God is breathing me."*

*Expand your awareness to include your whole body here in this present moment, as you tune in to all your senses – sight, sound, smell, touch, taste . . .*

*2) Say: "I let go of the past and the future, and embrace this eternal moment."*

*Breathe into this expanded always-new experience of the here and now . . .*

*3) Say: "I surrender my will to the higher good."*

*Now turn your focus to the feelings in your heart, right in the middle of your breathing experience, and say to yourself:*

*4) "I open my heart to receive God's love."*

*And as you stay aware of your breathing and your heart, say:*

*5) "I am quiet . . . and listening."*

*And when you're ready, open to a new experience as you say:*

*6) "I feel Jesus' presence in my heart."*

# Pause & Experience

# 21

# Serving God – With Pleasure

## Meditation 7: "I'm here to share love, light, and good times."

At some point, your inward meditative journey begins to come to a close, and your attention begins to turn outward to the environmental world again. At that moment, it's important to choose consciously to bring the depths of the meditation experience forward into your everyday life. This seventh step of the meditation involves staying focused on your breathing and the deep feelings in your heart, while opening your eyes and returning to regular activities.

As you might know from reading other books of mine, I'm in favor of seeing meditation not as something you do once or twice a day, but as an expanded state of consciousness that you learn to remain in, more and more of the time. If meditation means being purposefully aware, you can do this anytime, anywhere.

In my multi-tradition meditation text *Seven Masters, One Path* and my forthcoming business book *Take Charge of Your Mind,* I teach how even at work you can choose to be aware of your breathing and your heart, and bring spiritual qualities right into the heat of the workplace. Meditation in action is as important as meditation in peace and quiet.

So after each meditation session, as you begin to shift from inner contemplation and communion toward reengagement with the outside world, you'll want to learn how to carry with you the insights, peace, love, and wisdom that have come to you during meditation proper. To achieve this, all you need to do is first say a focus phrase that reflects what you want to bring to the world from your meditation: *"I'm here to share love, light, and good times."* Then as you open your eyes and go into action, continue to be aware of your breathing and your feelings in your heart, as you allow Spirit to act through you in all that you do.

## Holy Vehicle

The more I grow into my own understanding of spiritual life on this planet, the more I experience the truth that we are indeed the physical sensory eyes and ears of God, and that our deeper purpose is to allow Spirit to act through us in absolutely all that we do.

> When we behold God's beautiful creation, God experiences that creation through us. When we make love, God experiences, from the inside out, two of his creatures in deep sexual communion. Whatever we are experiencing in the present moment, God is experiencing this through us.

That's what it means to be spiritual: to choose in each new moment to be a conscious vehicle through which the higher dimensions of reality can enter mortal life and express the love and wisdom of the Creator.

How do you feel about this idea that God (upon invitation) will come and dwell within you and be one with you in what you do? Are you interested in truly surrendering your sense of individual ego primacy in order to participate in the greater transpersonal consciousness of the universe? I don't mean to be pushing my understanding here. Rather, I simply want to raise these possibilities so that you can consider them and explore their potential in your life. *Ideas* about the spiritual life only take us so far. What you're going to *experience* in the Jesus Spiral is just that: the experience of the truth of what this is all about.

And each time you emerge from formal meditation, you're going to carry the essence of your God encounter with you and share it. When you begin to emerge from meditation and say to yourself as the final expansion, *"I'm here to share love, light, and good times,"* you're simply stating your intent to bring with you what you've gained.

> Rather than leaving your spiritual gifts and insights in your meditation room, you're stating that your purpose is to share these gifts of love and insight and the wonderful feeling in your heart that comes from such an encounter with the divine.

## In-Action Meditation

Imagine you're at work, or out on a date, or doing something with your children, or even out struggling in sports or some physical hardship. What will happen if right in the middle of whatever you're doing, you remember to say, "God is breathing me," and tune in to that whole awakening process you're learning in this book for returning your attention fully to the present moment and awakening your feeling of having God in your heart? How will your life change if you develop the habit of saying one or more of the seven focus phrases you've learned herein and waking up to your spiritual power and presence everywhere you go?

I encourage you just to experiment. Right out of the blue sometimes, you can pause for a few breaths, and say to yourself, *"I feel Jesus's presence in my heart,"* or perhaps *"I surrender my will to the higher good."* Once you really learn these seven statements by heart, your heart will always have one of them ready to bring to the tip of your tongue, if only you pause now and then (the more often the better) and allow your attention to include this dimension of your spiritual life, right in the middle of the rest of your life.

Especially if you find yourself caught up in worrying all the time or being overly judgmental, as I described in depth in *Quiet Your Mind,* you can choose to shift directly out of downer thoughts and feelings into bright ones, through bringing to mind whatever focus phrase comes to you and holding this bright focus in your mind and heart as you continue with your day.

> Rather than letting your thoughts control you, you can control your thoughts, and choose to think thoughts that bring Spirit in! The choice, as we've seen throughout this book, is always yours: to remain contracted in your mind and closed in your heart or expansive in your mind and open in your heart.

The focus phrases and this entire meditation are here simply to help you accomplish that basic choice between the darkness and the light. Each new moment, will you slip into old judgmental and fear-based thoughts and feelings – or will you remember that you have the power to bring one of these focus phrases to mind and, by saying the words to yourself, wake up a brighter, more loving, spiritual state of mind?

# Reemerging

At some point in meditation, you will feel ready to return to everyday activities, and that's when you'll want to round it all off by saying, *"I am here to share love, light, and good times."* Perhaps you might come up with variations on this general theme of stating what you're really here on earth for. Sometimes, for instance, I say, "I'm here to serve, to prosper, and enjoy myself," or words to that general effect. The point is, as you return to everyday activities, clarify, deep down, the state of mind and heart you want to reemerge in.

> What I find most important is holding the choice of being filled with Spirit in everything I do, by realizing that each new inhalation is a chance to charge myself with life, love, and spiritual power.

The act of inhaling isn't just a physical act. It reflects our choice to inhale and bring into our being all dimensions of life, including the spiritual. Each new breath is an inflow that can carry God's presence – if that's what we consciously choose to do. Yes, it does require a bit of discipline in order to remember to say the focus phrases and point our attention toward spiritual experience. But as you'll find out for yourself, a bit of discipline isn't a negative duty; it's a positive doorway. Inertia often grabs our souls. We must act, and act again and again and again, to reawaken our spiritual consciousness.

And so, as you continue to memorize this basic meditation process (give yourself a couple of weeks of daily practice to get good at this and truly learn it by heart), here's the full process again.

# Meditation Expansion 7:

### "I am here to share love, light, and good times."

*Get comfortable . . . and turn your mind's full attention to the air flowing in and out of your nose . . . Expand your awareness to include the movements in your chest and belly . . . Exhale – hold – and then let your next inhale flow effortlessly in . . .*

*1) Say to yourself, "God is breathing me."*

*Expand your awareness to include your whole body here in this present moment, as you tune in to all your senses – sight, sound, smell, touch, taste . . .*

*2) Say: "I let go of the past and the future, and embrace this eternal moment."*

*Breathe into this expanded always-new experience of the here and now . . .*

*3) Say: "I surrender my will to the higher good."*

*Now turn your focus to the feelings in your heart, right in the middle of your breathing experience, and say to yourself:*

*4) "I open my heart to receive God's love."*

*And as you stay aware of your breathing and your heart, say:*

*5) "I am quiet . . . and listening."*

*And when you're ready, open to a new experience as you say:*

*6) "I feel Jesus' presence in my heart."*

*Allow your meditation to go where it naturally goes . . . for as long as it wants to go . . . and then when you're ready to reemerge into the everyday world, you can say to yourself:*

*7) "I am here to share love, light, and good times."*

*Stay with your breathing as central, especially when your eyes open on their own . . . and you go into action. With the feeling of Spirit and Jesus in your heart, the presence of God's will moving you spontaneously forward each new moment . . . go for it!*

 # Pause & Experience

**Final Words**

# The Jesus Spiral

I've given you hints here and there about this meditation being more than a one-shot linear process. Yes, you can move through the seven expansions just once when time is short, and a clear, beautiful, quick experience of your spiritual depths will come to you. I hope you pause and do this five to ten or even more times a day. In just seven breaths – one minute – you can actually experience the full meditation. And once you get good at the process, that one minute can be truly transforming in and of itself, be you on the subway, waiting for a meeting, standing in the shower, or any other place where you have a minute free. That free minute will shift your entire personal presence into spiritual empowerment and compassion.

When you have perhaps five or so minutes, you can go one step deeper, by moving through the meditation with a couple or three breaths for each of the seven expansion phrases – and then end with a couple of minutes of silent communion with the divine. At work, for instance, on your breaks, you can spend five minutes and bring Spirit into your workplace several times a day. Once you get good at carrying your meditative quality of consciousness with you after the meditation, you can literally spread light and God's love all the time at work.

> Finally, we come to the grand climax of this book and meditation process – when you have ten to 30 minutes free, and want to really go way deep. I do strongly encourage a daily meditation practice in which you devote a particular time slot in your day to meditation – up to half an hour set aside with reverence and diligence so that it becomes a solid daily part of your schedule.

There's nothing quite like the discipline of being a spiritually dedicated person who reserves at least half an hour a day for direct communion with the divine. Therefore, beyond the shorter versions of this Jesus meditation process, I heartily recommend the daily Jesus Spiral experience.

## The Jesus Spiral

Through experience, I've learned things about meditation over the last 30 years that run contrary to almost all traditional meditation methods. Traditionally, most meditations require that you focus your attention for long periods of time in one direction. The old logic was, the longer you held yourself in a particular meditation or mental fixation, the better and deeper the experience. But I've found that often just the opposite is true – at least for our contemporary personalities and mind-states.

> Specifically, I've found that moving through the basic seven-step expansion process several times in a fairly short time span is, for most people, more rewarding and easier

to stick with than trying to focus on just one theme or
meditation fixation for a longer period of time.

Yes, of course, a little discipline goes a long way in meditation and
spiritual evolution in general. But there's nothing holy, as far as I
can see, in forcing yourself to fix your attention rigidly and over-
long in one direction. Too often, all this does is generate a battle
between one part of your ego that says it's bored stiff and the sup-
posedly more spiritual side of your ego that insists on doing what
the meditation teacher said, even though it is boring you stiff.

Here's what I find that works much better all around. Yes,
have a bit of structure and discipline. Learn and then faithfully
employ the seven focus phrases each time you pause to meditate,
and, usually, discipline yourself to move through them in proper
order.

But rather than fixating on one of these expansions and
focus phrases for longer than a few breaths, it usually works best
to say the focus phrase, turn your mind's attention in that direction, and then, after just a breath or two or three, when you're
ready (and especially just before your mind starts to drift into
mundane thoughts and concerns), move on to the next expansion and say that focus phrase to yourself. After a few breaths (or
sometimes longer if you go deeply into that theme), go ahead
and say the next focus phrase that will expand your attention
even more.

> In other words, move through the entire expansion fairly
> quickly, so that you experience the full power of the
> process in one flow. This is, after all, an expansion process,
> so go all the way.

When you arrive at the sixth focus phrase and say, *"I feel Jesus'
presence in my heart,"* dwell with that experience for a few breaths.
Then, rather than trying to stay in whatever state you're in after
moving through the six expansions, do something truly liberating: Return to the first focus phrase, and say it a second time in

the same meditation. Then move through the entire six expansions again . . . and perhaps a third time . . . and even a fourth.

What happens when you turn the Jesus Meditation into the Jesus Spiral (round and round and up and up) is truly remarkable. I only discovered this dimensional expansion of the meditation process in my own life about a decade ago, but now I can't imagine meditating in any other way – because it works so well, and makes meditation not only effortless, but a natural flow that is a pure joy.

## Exponential Expansions

Here's psychologically what seems to be happening with the Jesus Spiral that makes the spiritual experience so exponentially expansive. The first time you say one of the focus phrases, you'll find that yes, you go a certain distance, but that's all. If you stay with that first step too long you'll pop out of meditation altogether, or have to employ bothersome discipline to hold your attention there.

> But if you move on to the next phrase fairly quickly, your ego continues to feel engaged (it has its important role to play, remembering your lines!) and your focus of attention looks in a somewhat new direction that will always be interesting – for a certain amount of time, until you process what comes to you with that expansion.

Then, before too long, you will find that you naturally want to move into the next expansion – and that's what expanding is all about! Fairly soon, you come to the sixth expansion, and rather than saying the seventh focus phrase that ends the meditation, you say the first focus phrase again.

You'll discover that when you turn your attention to that first expansion a second time in the same meditation, you return to that expansion where you left it and go deeper, because you've expanded your consciousness with the other expansions in the meanwhile. And so, each time you move through the six expansions, you spiral higher. The second time around, the experience will be exponentially stronger. This might be subtle, but it's always true. And the third and fourth time that you say, for instance, "I open my heart to receive God's love," the experience of the inflow will be dramatically deeper than the first time you said the same focus phrase in this meditation.

> What I'm handing you right now is perhaps the most important insight I've had into meditation – certainly one of the most dramatic in my life. A seemingly simple step-by-step meditation can become a spiral that lifts you higher and higher.

You'll find that on the second and third and fourth rounds on the spiral, you might naturally want to shorten some of the focus phrases a bit, as your thoughts become quieter and deeper – like this:

*"God is breathing me."*
*"I embrace the eternal now."*
*"I surrender to the higher good."*
*"I open my heart."*
*"I am quiet."*
*"I feel Jesus' presence."*

## Top of the Spiral

At some point, perhaps on the second round you make on the Jesus Spiral, perhaps on the third or fourth, occasionally on the fifth, you'll reach a special point where your ego says a focus phrase to you and then falls silent, and you enter into a word-less deep meditation on that particular theme and expansion. Your ego totally disappears and you are silent and at one with your Creator.

> Like a spiritual roulette wheel, you spin the six meditation themes and their focus phrases, and go round and round on the spiral . . . until the wheel stops spinning, and you are pointed with your full attention in exactly the direction that Spirit has chosen for your meditation focus that day.

For instance, perhaps your personal ego is recently acting a bit out of hand and pushing its selfish agenda in your life, rather than surrendering to your deeper voice of wisdom. In this case, you might find that you progress a few times around the Jesus Spiral, then say a final time to yourself, *"I surrender my will to the higher good,"* and move deeply into meditation on this experience, as God's love and wisdom expand your personal stance a beautiful step.

Whatever the last focus phrase you say on the Spiral, you will enter into deep wordless meditation at that point. I of course have no idea what will happen in your meditation. Nor can you know until you open yourself in that moment, and experience what comes to you.

That's the ultimate beauty of such a meditation process: It's always new. There's never a repeat performance in the eternal present moment. We are participating in the great unfolding of God's creation, each new moment. And all we can do is tune in to the experience, open our hearts to God's inspiration, and participate with all our hearts, minds, and souls.

Having said all that, my words are coming to an end in this book. Enough said. You have the meditation tools now in hand. You can go online for further training or return to the beginning of this book and go deeper into the mastery of the seven expansions. All in all, this has been a most insightful and enjoyable chat with you about Spirit. I've been doing this basic meditation all through the writing of this book, and certainly couldn't have even begun the book without Spirit's inspiration and wisdom.

I thank you for moving with me through this exploration – and I feel connected with you in Spirit as we continue to share this eternal moment. Blessings on your spiritual journey!

## The Jesus Spiral

*"God is breathing me."*
*"I let go of the past and future, and embrace this eternal moment."*
*"I surrender my will to the higher good."*
*"I open my heart to receive God's love."*
*"I am quiet . . . and listening."*
*"I feel Jesus' presence in my heart."*
~
*"God is breathing me."*
*"I embrace the eternal now."*
*"I surrender to the higher good."*
*"I open my heart to God's love."*
*"I am quiet . . . and listening."*
*"I feel Jesus' presence."*
~
*"God is breathing me."*
*"I embrace the eternal now."*
*"I surrender."*
*"I open my heart."*
*"I am quiet. "*
*"I feel Jesus' presence."*
~
*"I am here to share love, light, and good times."*

# Making All This Your Own

You have now read through this book and have a general idea of how to approach this new meditation and spiritual-awakening process. What happens now? So many people read one inspiring book, put it aside and pick up another, and never quite break through the talk-about phase of spiritual awakening. They never advance into a genuine inner practice that delivers meaningful results in their lives. I want to encourage you right here, right now, to move beyond "seeking" and become a "finder."

The experience of spiritual awakening isn't found in books; it's found inside your heart and soul. Even this present book, which focuses on pragmatic tools for finding spiritual solace and insight, doesn't hold the experience you're seeking. Therefore what you do next is of vital importance. Please observe yourself, your thoughts, and your behavior after finishing this book – are you ready to shift and choose to be not a seeker, but a finder?

You've now found pragmatic meditation tools that will point your mind's attention directly toward the actual experience that

Jesus was pointing his followers toward. But in the same way that Jesus didn't force people to look in the directions he pointed, this book doesn't force you to use meditation tools derived from Jesus' teachings to wake up your inner light.

> The focus is on you now. You have the tools in hand. You can close the book, put the tools aside, and continue being a seeker – or you can now begin to discipline yourself (just a bit) to memorize this seven-step Jesus Meditation process, move through the actual process often each day, and shift from thinking about to experiencing yourself as a conscious spiritual being.

I know that it's not easy to shift from being a thinker to being a doer. Our entire civilization works against the meditative process; every spare minute we have tends to get sucked up by the media rather than used effectively for inner awakening and healing.

Therefore I've developed the best support and training system currently possible, so that if you want help, help is at hand. First of all, this book itself is the primary in-hand vehicle for genuinely learning the Jesus Meditation method by heart. Just go back to the first chapter, go deep into the discussion, and, especially, memorize the focus phrase and make it your own.

> Proceed through each chapter and this time truly come to know the process as your own. Feel free to copy any page you want to have in hand, so you can post it at work, in your bedroom, in the kitchen – make the focus phrases as visible as you can in your life. And move through the process until it becomes a new positive habit.

Also feel free to go on your computer to my primary online teaching site found at www.johnselby.com and take advantage of the programs, forums, readings, audio uplifts, and e-courses you'll find there, both for this method and for related programs that will nurture your soul. You'll find me available to answer your questions at the various forums, and my voice is always ready through streamed audio and CD programs to guide you through the method until you truly learn it by heart. See you there!

# About the Author

**JOHN SELBY** grew up on a cattle ranch in California, went to Princeton University and Berkeley, and then the San Francisco Theological Seminary. He completed psychological research at the National Institutes of Health integrating meditation and cognitive science, before turning to private therapy and spiritual counseling work. Married with three children, he has recently developed at-work methods and online audio-training programs for instant access to his teachings and courses.

He can be reached at **www.johnselby.com**.

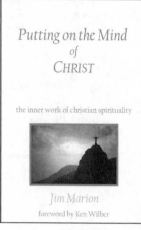
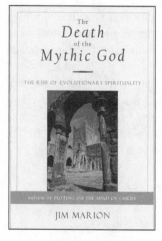